Appleby Gypsy Horse Fair:
Mythology, Origins, Evolution and Evaluation

Appleby Gypsy Horse Fair:
Mythology, Origins, Evolution and Evaluation

Andrew Connell

CUMBERLAND AND WESTMORLAND
ANTIQUARIAN AND ARCHAEOLOGICAL SOCIETY
2015

Cumberland and Westmorland
Antiquarian and Archaeological Society
Hon. General Editor
Professor Colin Richards

Appleby Gypsy Horse Fair:
Mythology, Origins, Evolution and Evaluation

EXTRA SERIES NO. XLIV

ISBN 978 1 873124 68 0

Printed by
Titus Wilson & Son, Kendal
2015

Contents

List of Figures

Forewords

Country fairs have been a feature of the English rural scene since medieval times. They have played an important part in shaping local economies and communal life, and in reinforcing or creating a sense of local identity. But many of the accounts of them tend to be largely descriptive or even anecdotal. This history of the famous 'Horse Fair' at Appleby in Westmorland by Andrew Connell is scrupulously scholarly yet also highly accessible, and therefore warmly to be welcomed. The author is both a trained historian (I was his tutor at The Queen's College, Oxford) and also at the time of writing mayor of the town of Appleby. So he is exceptionally well qualified from every point of view to provide the informative and balanced analysis that Appleby Fair deserves.

The author shows how the Fair evolved over the centuries. As he demonstrates, suggestions that it owed its origins to a royal charter from James II in 1685 are without substance. But in the mid-eighteenth century, partly as a result of dispute between prominent local landed families, a 'New Fair' was established. It then went through many mutations. Originally a market for the sale of agricultural livestock, it was successively a drovers' fair, a horse fair and, by 1914, a colourful and vibrant fair for the Gypsy/Travelling community who would assemble around the quiet, small Westmorland town for a few days in early June every year, bringing their vivid culture with them. In the period after the Second World War the original horse fair became perhaps more of a media fair, often sentimentalized as 'the world's biggest gypsy party', but in June 2014, despite recurrent controversy, it was still going strong.

Andrew Connell tells us much in passing of the cultural attributes and reputation of the Romany people and how they impacted on Appleby residents. He also shows how, inevitably perhaps, there was some cultural conflict with the local community, with resistance to the disorder and disturbance of which they were accused by journalists and right-wing politicians, and with attempts to bring this traditional event to an end. Local authorities argued with one other. But the book also shows how in the 1960s the Romany people successfully regrouped in appealing that their fair should survive, and how they managed to return to the traditional site on Fair Hill. On balance, the survival of this ancient annual folk festival is a tribute to the tolerance and open-mindedness of the people of Appleby who have appreciated the colour and drama the Gypsy fair brought into their lives for a brief interlude – 'the most important event on the calendar', 'a romantic, magical place where you courted and met your future lifelong partner'. It is a notable landmark in the social experience of this beautiful region of England, and Andrew Connell's meticulous account of its fascinating history deserves the widest readership.

Kenneth O. Morgan
House of Lords
4 July 2014
(Professor Lord Morgan is Visiting Professor at King's College, London, and an Honorary Fellow of The Queen's College, Oxford).

Andrew Connell's fascinating account of how Appleby Fair came into being and has sustained itself since is required reading. His background as a trained historian has prepared him well for this forensic examination of the roots of this world-famous fair, as well as his role as the local mayor, where he has defended the fair and promoted social cohesion between the travelling communities who frequent it and the townsfolk who host it. As a frequent visitor to this fair – which has become, as the Gypsy elder Billy Welch calls it, "sacred ground" to the Gypsy and Traveller people, I hope it remains part of the Cumbrian calendar forever.

Katharine Quarmby
London
21 January 2015
(Katharine Quarmby is a journalist and author who has worked with, and written extensively about, Gypsy/Travellers in contemporary Britain).

Author's Preface and Acknowledgements

I first became aware of Appleby Fair in 1973, when I took charge of the history department at Appleby Grammar School. Full-time teaching at a comprehensive school is quite demanding, however; and when a switch to part-time working did enable me to do serious archival research, the initial focus of my published work was political, as will be apparent from some of the references in this book. It was only after becoming an Appleby town councillor in 2006 that I gave much thought to the origins of the Fair, began to question some of the general assumptions about it, and somewhat to my surprise discovered that, although one or two starts had been made, no scholarly work had been published. Membership of Eden District Council from 2011, representing Bongate, in which most of the Fair activity takes place, further concentrated the mind.

The journey of exploration has taken me to some unexpected places with unexpected results: as Euripidean choruses would say, 'the things we thought would happen do not happen'. I believe I have gained greater understanding of the people who come to Appleby Fair, the people who reside in the surrounding area and those who labour in local government; it is not, of course, the historian's business to moralise, but on balance I think rather better of my fellow-human beings than I previously did. My conclusions are, I hope, soundly based and sufficient to present a clear and fair picture; I think that most books (and, indeed, films and songs) are longer than they need be. But rash indeed would be the historian who claimed to have said the last word on this or any other subject.

My gratitude is due to my wife and children for their forbearance with my protracted preoccupations. Many other good people have helped me with advice, assistance and encouragement. Others did so inadvertently: their justified concerns about the status of public access to the Fair Hill forced me, in my mayoral capacity, to seek out previously ignored documents and press reports, with wonderful results. I would like to thank Thomas Acton, Dot Anderton, Richard Atkinson, Sue Bradley, Mary Burnside, Graham Coles, David Cressy, Jane Dawson, Pippa Dewis, Caroline Dodgeon, Vivienne Gate, Charles Hirst, Ian Holloway, Sarah Holloway, Robin Hooper, Anthony Hothfield, Pam Kelly, Ella Langan, Elaine Lomas, David Lowis, Andrew Lund, Barry McKay, Keith Morgan, Kenneth Morgan, Judith Okely, Alice Palmer, Rachel Pearson, Hughie Potts, Katharine Quarmby, Peter Roebuck, Rachel Smith, Rory Stewart, Mally Taylor, John Tillotson, Billy Welch, Kay Whitehead and the staffs of Appleby Tourist Information Centre, Kendal Archive Centre, Leeds University Library Special Collections, the British

Library and the Appleby, Kendal and Penrith branches of the Cumbria County Library Service. I ask anyone inadvertently missed from the list above to accept my apologies.

Above all, my grateful thanks go to Colin Richards, a most perceptive and understanding series editor, whose advice has been sound, prompt and unequivocal; and to Bryan Harper, who handled production and printing with good-humoured, easy-going efficiency. I owe them much.

Andrew (Andy) Connell
Appleby-in-Westmorland
19 March 2015

Chapter 1:

'The world's biggest gathering of gypsies'

In 2013 the *Sun* told its readers, not for the first time, that Appleby Fair was 'the world's biggest gathering of gypsies, dating back to 1685'.[1] Such assertions should be treated with some scepticism. This study will show that, on the basis of the available evidence, the stated date of the origin of what is now known as Appleby Fair is demonstrably wrong, and its identity as a gathering of Gypsy/Travellers evolved only gradually. Whether by the twenty-first century it had become the largest gathering of its kind on the planet is a claim incapable of proof and beyond the scope of the pages that follow.

Fairs are by their nature intense, transient events, liable to invoke extreme reactions: for those who take part they may bring exhilaration or disappointment; to those who look on they may appear exotic or disgusting

Figure 1. River Eden during Appleby Fair, 2014. Photographer: Keith Morgan; reproduced with his kind permission.

---

1   *Sun*, 10 Jun. 2013. Throughout this book direct quotations from sources are left as published, although it is now customary for 'Gypsy' and 'Traveller' to be capitalised. The extent to which these are distinct designations is a moot point; I have in this study preferred the descriptor, 'Gypsy/Traveller'.

(Figure 1). Historical surveys of English fairs have tended to be descriptive, wistful evocations of a colourful, bustling, lusty world, for the most part lost or debased beyond recall.[2] The assessment by J.A. Chartres in a study more academically orientated than most would command general acceptance: 'as commercial institutions of significance the open market and the fair in England were dead by the third quarter of the nineteenth century'.[3] They had been in the main a medieval development to facilitate the marketing of livestock, especially cattle. Some were established under the aegis of a town's chartered market rights, some by virtue of a charter granted to a noble family or a monastic house; the origins of other fairs were simply obscure. Fairs continued to develop until the late eighteenth century; in 1792 there were said to be 1,515 in England.[4] But by the mid-Victorian era great gatherings like those at Scarborough and St. Bartholomew's in Smithfield had passed into history and such vade mecums for travelling salesmen as Ogilby's *Traveller's Pocket Book* and Owen's *New Book of Fairs*, compendiums listing locations, dates and routes, had ceased publication. Such formerly thriving inland fairs as Horncastle in Lincolnshire and Stourbridge in Cambridgeshire were spectres of their former selves that would barely limp into the twentieth century. The reasons were various: macadamized roads, canals, railways and steamships all encouraged the development of large, permanent retail outlets and reduced the need for fairs; the growing temperance movement found the licentiousness traditionally associated with them morally repugnant; and the 1871 Fairs Act facilitated closure by local magistrates, with the agreement of the Home Secretary.[5]

'That which was least wholesome remained to the end', darkly remarked the Rev. N.F. Hulbert in his 1936 survey of Somerset fairs.[6] He perhaps had in mind Bridgwater Fair, still held in late September. Said to have originated as a sheep fair chartered by King John, it is now promoted by Sedgemoor District Council as the largest funfair in southwest England,[7] but does not attract the media attention or the endemic controversy that have become part and parcel of Appleby Fair. To be sure, 'horse fairs would endure better than most',[8] but the continuing rude health of the Appleby gathering contrasts with the virtual demise of nearby Brough Hill Fair, similarly associated with Gypsy/Travellers and within living memory an event of comparable

2   W. Addison, *English Fairs and Markets* (London, 1953) includes a bibliography, but no notes; D. K. Cameron, *The English Fair* (Stroud, 1998) has neither.

3   J.A. Chartres, *Markets, Fairs and the Community in 17ᵗʰ and 18ᵗʰ Century England* (University of Leeds School of Economic Studies Discussion Paper, 1974).

4   *Agrarian History of England & Wales* (Cambridge, repr. 2011), vol. IV, pp. 532-41, A.M. Everitt; V, pp. 420-442, VI, p. 223, J.A. Chartres.

5   Cameron, *English Fair*, pp. 209-234.

6   N. Hulbert, 'A Survey of the Somerset fairs', *Proceedings of the Somerset Archaeological and Natural History Society*, LXXXII (1936), pp. 83-159.

7   www.sedgemoor.gov.uk/index.aspx?articleid=5860, accessed 18 October 2013.

8   Cameron, *English Fair*, p. 227.

status. Speculative head counts of visitors to the present-day horse fairs at Barnet, Stow-in-the-Wold or Lee Gap are computed in hundreds, Appleby's in thousands. The following chapters will sketch the Appleby Fair of the present day; examine the extent to which the mythology surrounding its origins corresponds with the evidence; explain its evolution from a sheep and cattle drovers' gathering to a horse fair and the changing part played in it by Gypsy/Travellers; and discuss the way in which the reluctant involvement of local authorities with the Fair inadvertently contributed to its modern status as a media event.

The exercise is not without its problems. Patrons of Appleby Fair in its various manifestations over more than two centuries have left little in writing; there are only a handful of relevant documents and letters. Almost all printed sources, often highly subjective, have been produced by onlookers. The oral testimony of participants presents the usual problems of uncertain location of time and place: particular incidents are generalised and things that happen twice have 'always' happened. Uncompromising individual opinions are liable to misinterpretation as being representative of a whole community. Moreover, any discussion of the growing role of Gypsy/Travellers will run into problems of definition. Though the word 'Gypsy' derived from the notion that those to whom it was applied were of Egyptian descent, the framers of laws penalising Gypsies across Europe from the sixteenth to the twentieth centuries in practice struggled with the competing claims of ethnicity, culture and appearance in clarifying precisely whom it was they wished to exclude or even – during World War II – wipe out.[9] Modern scholars, usually with the benign intent of understanding rather than vilifying marginalised groups, have faced similar dilemmas. Not all accept the view, essentially based on linguistic analysis, that 'North-west India formed the cradle of the Romany nation'.[10] Angus Fraser, a civil servant turned historian, postulated a succession of migrations between c. 300 B.C. and c. 1200 A.D. that brought Gypsies into western Europe;[11] but the anthropologist Michael Stewart, highlighting the paucity of documentary evidence for these movements, followed his mentor Judith Okely in preferring a sociological, quasi-Marxist explanation.[12] This emphasises the process by which Gypsies evolved out of 'the landless poor who had refused to become proletarians' when confronted by societal upheaval: the decay of feudalism, the rise of capitalism, the Highland clearances, the evictions following the Irish potato famine, and the collapse of socialism in Eastern Europe.[13] In this model '"Gypsiness" is continually made possible

---

9   D. Kenrick & G. Puxon, *Gypsies under the Swastika* (Hatfield, 1995), pp. 9-48. For definitions of Gypsies in modern English law, D. Kenrick & C. Clark, *Moving On* (Hatfield, 1999), pp. 148-55.

10   Kenrick & Clark, *Moving On*, p. 24.

11   A. Fraser, *The Gypsies* (Oxford, 1992), pp. 33-83; Y. Matras, *I Met Lucky People* (London 2014) pp. 1-30.

12   J. Okely, *The Traveller-Gypsies* (London, 1983)

13   M. Stewart, *The Time of the Gypsies* (Oxford, 1997), pp. 236-238.

by the nature of our societies ... even if the *gázos* assimilated all the Gypsies, they would re-invent themselves.'[14]

'With their gaze fixed on a permanent present that is always becoming a timeless now',[15] most Gypsy/Travellers are not much given to speculation on their origins. They know how to describe themselves and their circle and have a range of names for those with whom they do not identify; but these are 'heavily contested'.[16] Outsiders may attempt to engage with insider categorisation, listing 'different strands of the British and Irish travelling nation ... English Rom and Sinti, English, Irish and Scots Travellers, Welsh Gypsies and many shades of wannabes and in-betweens'.[17] Or they may employ dismissive terminology, ranging from the intentionally derogatory 'gyppo' and 'pikey' to the merely arcane, as when in 1987 in a letter to the local newspaper some Appleby shopkeepers protested 'emphatically' that they did not raise their prices 'when the potters visit the town'.[18] Applied to nineteenth-century Gypsy/Travellers such as those based at Natland, near Kendal,[19] the term denoted people who acquired earthenware 'seconds' from ceramic factories and travelled round the country with horse and cart, selling them at markets and fairs; it survived long after the practice ceased. A century later the veteran Cumbrian gypsiologist T.W. Thompson defined 'potters' as:

> ...a nomadic or semi-nomadic caste, found mainly in Cumberland, Westmorland and Furness, who had some Gypsy blood in their veins, and a fair sprinkling of words of Roman origin in their cant, and who evidently hawked earthenware at one time, but have not done so for the past hundred years or more.[20]

A more persistent trope has been the supposed difference between the acceptable 'real Gypsies', who in some indeterminate golden age dignified Appleby Fair, and the parvenu 'riff-raff' who, as one letter from a resident to the press complained in 1986, now 'foul our streets' with their 'barbaric behaviour'.[21] Even though Gypsy/Travellers themselves will sometimes talk in such terms, Okely's survey based on extensive fieldwork in the early 1970s insisted that 'the very notion of the "real" Gypsy raises more questions than

---

14   Ibid., p. 238. *Gázos* ('full of wind') is the name applied to non-Gypsies by Hungarian Gypsy/Travellers, cf. gorgio, gadje etc.
15   Ibid., p. 243. Though specific to Hungarian Rom, this is a persuasive generalisation.
16   C. Clark, 'Who are the Gypsies and Travellers?' in *Here to Stay: the Gypsies & Travellers of Britain* ed. C. Clark & M. Greenfields (Hatfield, 2006), p. 11. Matras, *Lucky People* makes a clear distinction between Roms and Travellers, and treats 'Gypsy' as an externally imposed label.
17   R. Sagar-Musgrave, *Appleby Fair: the Greatest Gypsy and Traveller Gathering* (London, 2011), introduction by Bill Lloyd.
18   *Cumberland & Westmorland Herald*, 13 Jun. 1987.
19   *Lonsdale Magazine*, vol. II, XXII (Sep. 1821), pp. 343-347.
20   T.W. Thompson, *Wordsworth's Hawkshead* (Oxford, 1970).
21   *Herald* 21 Jun. 1986.

answers';[22] Colin Clark agrees that dichotomies defined in racial or moral terms – 'the "proper" or "deserving" Gypsy' as opposed to the '"pretend and "undeserving" traveller' – are 'bogus'.[23] But the distinction undoubtedly continues to have widespread currency, even if some of the evidence for this proves to be equally unsound. In an earlier publication Clark quoted the former Conservative Home Office minister David Maclean, whose constituency included Appleby, as having told the Commons on 26 July 1993 that the controversial Criminal Justice and Public Order Act was not aimed at 'the genuine Romany or other Gypsies'.[24] It is evident from a trawl through *Hansard*, however, that Maclean did not in fact say anything about Gypsy/Travellers in the House on that or any other date. The subject seems to have been the preserve of Charles Wardle, a ministerial colleague.

This surprising discovery is a useful reminder that although scholarship, the law, and society in general – in marked contrast to Gypsy/Travellers themselves – place greater credence in written than in oral sources, the appearance of a statement in print has never been a guarantee of its authenticity. Newspapers of the eighteenth and nineteenth centuries were as prone to garbling stories as their present-day counterparts; and the modern practice of cutting and pasting from often carelessly assembled websites was foreshadowed by the way in which compilers of almanacks and directories would reproduce and perpetuate one another's mistakes. This study inevitably relies primarily on surviving paper sources; but it will argue that the apparent information found therein is not necessarily – and in some instances cannot possibly be – true.

---

22   Okely, *Traveller-Gypsies*, p. 1.
23   Clark, 'Conclusion', *Here to Stay*, pp. 281-3.
24   Idem, '"New Age" Travellers: identity, sedentarism and social security' in *Gypsy politics and Traveller identity*, ed. T. Acton (Hatfield, 1997), p.137.

Chapter 2:

Appleby Fair, 2013: 'an injection of colour'

The rhythms and melodies of Appleby Fair have changed over time. The date of what is now generally acknowledged to be Britain's largest horse fair was for two centuries at least the second Wednesday in June; but in 2013, following the pattern of recent years, it began on the preceding Thursday, activity peaked on Saturday, and by Monday 10 June, two days before its putative climax, it was effectively over. Under warm sunshine and blue skies 1301 caravans, 178 of them horse-drawn bow-tops,[1] occupied pitches in fields to the north of Westmorland's former county town. Most of the estimated 5,000 or more occupants would acknowledge the designation 'Gypsy/Traveller'.[2] Generally in family groups, they had come to meet up with old friends – or in some cases enemies – and make new ones, largely from among their own sub-group: interaction between Travellers from the Thames estuary, north-east England and Ireland, for example, is limited, and those who consider themselves Romani tend to keep their own company.[3]

Figure 2. Tranquillity on Fair Hill. Photographer: Tom Green; reproduced with his kind permission.

---

1   For the cultural significance of bow-tops to Appleby Fair, see D. Smith, 'Gypsy aesthetics, identity and creativity: the painted wagon' in T. Acton & G. Mundy eds., *Romani culture and Gypsy identity* (Hatfield, 1997).

2   Caravans (usually called 'trailers' by Gypsy/Travellers) are counted by Eden District Council, to which should be added vans and other vehicles in which people slept in order to estimate the total traveller population on the basis of 3-4 people per carrier.

3   On the Fair Hill the Roma flag flew. It was evident from conversation that those on the Fair Hill would no more dream of camping elsewhere than would the occupants of other fields consider moving there.

Figure 3. The Sands, Appleby, on the Friday of the Fair 2007. Photographer: Keith Morgan; reproduced with his kind permission.

Some fairgoers spent their short holiday mainly around their caravans, exchanging gossip and preparing leisurely family meals in front of a backdrop of the sunbathed Pennines a few miles to the east (Figure 2). Others thronged into the town to mingle in the crowds and consume fast food supplied by an array of shops and stalls. They neither created nor were offered much organised entertainment: there were no roundabouts or street musicians. While older Travellers watched the world go by, the younger ones engaged in a perpetual parade. Young women, elaborately coiffeured, made-up and bedecked with jewellery, displaying much tanned skin emerging from skimpy garments, generally of white or various fluorescent hues,[4] strode out confidently on high heels, gossiped, shopped for souvenirs and queued for toilets. Young men, their neatly gelled hair usually not covered by the caps and hats that their elders still favour, often bare chested, sometimes – a recent trend – bare legged, brandished switches and knowingly inspected horses, which they periodically mounted to trot with apparent purpose amidst the crowds. Several hundred horses, bred to pull carts and bow-top caravans or race in harness, had been brought to the fair, most in transporters, but a few on foot. The horses were shown off, put through their paces on various stretches of road, carefully washed in the River Eden as crowds looked on

---

4   In marked contrast to earlier generations of Gypsy/Traveller women, whose clothing, though colourful, had not to be revealing; this serves as a corrective to perceptions of ossified social customs.

(Figure 1); some were traded. Often, hitched to convenient railings and lamp posts, they had to pass hours patiently waiting while a tide of predominantly male humanity surged – often at the summons of a mobile phone call – in and out of Appleby's several pubs, thirsty for lager out of the plastic glasses that have become mandatory for the Fair's duration.

By day Gypsy/Traveller numbers were at least doubled by visitors: some had Traveller connections, most came to see the sights and absorb the atmosphere or seek bargains in the recently-established Market Field from stalls whose wares ranged from horse brasses to CDs of Irish crooners. Like the Gypsy/Travellers themselves, visitors arrived mainly in cars and vans, crawling along gridlocked roads to grassy areas enterprisingly converted to temporary car parks; some came by coach, several hundred by train. On a rough calculation based on a sample of the occupancy of car parks, assuming the average vehicle load to be four, along with a count of coaches and estimates of passengers alighting from trains at Appleby station, perhaps 12,000 people came in and out of the town on the Saturday. The often-quoted figure of 20,000 or 30,000 in a day is based on no known evidence; the occasionally-mentioned 50,000 might approximate to the accumulated number of people over a whole fair. Some of the town's population of 3,050 joined the crowds, or interacted with them through retailing; others preferred to avoid the streets, shops and pubs while the fair lasted.

The location for the greatest density of humans and horses was The Sands, a broad highway abutting the river bank and overlooked by the town bridge (Figure 3). Here too was the main concentration of high-visibility jacketed police officers; over a hundred were around the town at peak times to keep traffic moving and maintain public order. The atmosphere was largely good-humoured, with only a handful of arrests for drunk and disorderly conduct and minor acts of violence; but on Friday 7 June 2013 the police did apprehend more than twenty men heading for Appleby Fair Hill with intent to inflict grievous bodily harm or worse on various enemies. This was a Gypsy/Traveller issue, and the arrests were witnessed by few; but later that day there was highly public drama. A stolen car pursued by police forced its way through the crowds, injuring pedestrians and a horse before becoming wedged in a vain attempt to get between a low house wall and the rear of a loaded school bus positioned diagonally, at the request of the police, to block the road. Instant rumours that the driver was a Gypsy bound for Fair Hill, who had shot at police before his capture, were not true; and the children on the bus were unhurt and mostly unperturbed, despite subsequent national newspaper stories that they had been screaming in terror.[5] The arrested

---

5   *Daily Mail, Daily Telegraph* , 13 Jun. 2013. I saw and spoke to some of the children a few minutes after they had been led from the bus to wait for a replacement in the library of nearby Appleby Grammar School, where I was a teacher. I felt that I had gauged the general mood, in advance of the media attention that the incident for various reasons attracted.

driver pleaded guilty to dangerous driving, driving without a licence or insurance and handling stolen goods, and was given a prison sentence at Carlisle Crown Court on 8 July: he had no connection with Appleby Fair and had detoured into the town in an attempt to shake off his pursuers.

Neither of these incidents was mentioned in the first report of the 2013 fair to appear in the *Sun*; it focused instead on blonde Irish Traveller Sammie Jo, worried that at 18 she might be left on the shelf and 'on the prowl' for a suitable husband. There were, *Sun* readers learned, many more like her: the 'quiet streets' of 'the sleepy, picturesque market town in Cumbria' were 'awash with hotpants, boob tubes, crop tops and skintight micro-dresses'. Residents generally seemed, despite 'some grumbles, ... to welcome the fair as an injection of colour into their otherwise quiet lives'.[6] The same might reasonably have been said in the wake of the 2014 Fair, which produced no headline-grabbing incident. That year the recorded number of bow-top caravans rose, but after a busy Friday heavy Saturday rain discouraged some visitors. More Gypsy/Travellers seemed to have brought their children, a trend reflected in growing numbers of small boys driving sulkies drawn by Shetland ponies, which were reportedly at a premium in horse sales; and in a revival of live outdoor music, with girls to fore (Figures 4-5).

As the Fair came to an end a cameraman repeated an exercise carried out in 2013 by taking satisfying pictures of muddy ruts and piles of rubbish in camping areas to accompany a *Daily Mail* report of 'beautiful Cumbrian hillsides and green pastures . . . left spoiled with overflowing skips, bags of litter, abandoned furniture and broken loos . . . while debris trails through the land where the lush green grass once stood'.[7] The general local consensus, however, was that the clean-up was swift and efficient; within days there were, as usual, few visible signs that the Fair had ever happened.

---

6   *Sun*, 10 Jun. 2013.

7   *Daily Mail On-line*, 11 June 2014: 'Thousands of travellers decamp from Appleby and THIS is the mess they left behind.' Remarkably, *Daily Mail On-line*, 12 June 2014, reported that travellers from Appleby Fair had been in Gunnersbury Park, North London, for the past three days, leaving behind 50 tons of rubbish including at least one smashed piano. Their speed of movement when so heavily laden was not discussed.

Figure 4. Street Entertainment, 2014. Photograph by Keith Morgan; reproduced with his kind permission.

Figure 5. Entertainment on Fair Hill in preparation, 2014. Photograph by Keith Morgan; reproduced with his kind permission.

Chapter 3:
Mythology: the Phantom Charter

Such interest on the part of national media in the sights, sounds and perspectives of Appleby Fair is relatively recent; so is speculation about its origins. Victorian local press reports were generally content to record that it had 'always been considered a great fair and well attended',[1] before turning to its importance in 'regulating the price of stock'.[2] A century later, however, 'the world's greatest gypsy gathering' was represented as a 'time-honoured ritual' which had, the *Guardian* reported in 1991, begun in 1685 when James II granted the town a charter conveying on it the right to hold the fair: 'Three centuries later the gypsies are still taking him at his word'.[3] The king could not have known, remarked a 1998 history of English fairs, 'the forces he was about to unleash on the loyal citizenry'.[4] This tale was not new: in 1980 the *Lancashire Evening Post* described Appleby Horse Fair as 'granted a Royal Charter by James II in 1685 and roping in itinerants by the thousand ever since'.[5] In 1985 on the Sunday of the Fair, the usual attempts to confine horses to the north side of the Eden were relaxed and a colourful procession of horse-drawn vehicles and ponies paraded up Boroughgate, Appleby's main street. The mayor handed out rosettes in commemoration of the tercentenary of the Fair, although the local press report did sound a cautionary note that 'this is much disputed'.[6]

Certainly, many English fairs originated with a royal charter, usually conferred on an institution or an individual. Brough Hill Fair owed its existence to a charter granted to Robert, Lord Clifford in 1330 by Edward III;[7] the fairs in May and October at Stow-on-the Wold have been traced to a charter granted to Evesham Abbey by Edward IV in 1476.[8] By then Appleby was an old-established borough, having secured the right of corporate self-government in 1179 by a charter of Henry II, a brief document which simply stated that the town had the same rights as York. The charter was renewed at irregular intervals up to 1628, without significant additions. By 1587 – and probably for centuries before – Appleby Corporation was accustomed

---

1   *Kendal Mercury*, 16 Jun. 1849.
2   *Westmorland Gazette*, 16 Jun. 1849
3   *Guardian*, 11 May 1991, 'The fairest fair of all'.
4   Cameron, *English Fair*, p. 100.
5   *Lancashire Evening Post*, 14 Jun. 1980.
6   *Herald*, 15 Jun. 1985
7   W. Whellan, *History of Cumberland and Westmorland* (London, 1860), p. 730.
8   C R. Elvington, ed., *Victoria County History*, History of Gloucestershire vol. 6 (1965), pp. 165-72.

to host, in addition to regular markets, a Whit Monday fair,[9] one of whose functions was the hiring of domestic servants and farm labourers.[10] These were evidently held by prescriptive right: none of the Appleby charters, eleven by 1628, mentioned markets or fairs.

Yet Tudor Appleby, still not fully recovered from destruction by invading Scots in 1388, remained, in the words of its recent historian, a 'Depressed Area' until its extensive mid-seventeenth century restoration by the formidable Lady Anne Clifford, who died in 1676.[11] Within a decade of her death a chartered fair was indeed conferred on Appleby Corporation, but this royal grant was not a local favour but part of wider issues of national politics. The determination of Charles II that the protracted drama of the 1679-80 Exclusion Parliaments and the spectre of renewed civil war should never be repeated led to parliamentary boroughs being systematically subjected to *quo warranto* inquests. They were required to surrender their charters of incorporation and accept new ones, very different in form; in these the King assumed the power to remove corporation members whenever he chose, and thereby the means to control future parliamentary elections. To make this more palatable, some boroughs – Hereford for example – were authorised to hold new fairs.[12]

But the wholesale re-issuing of charters was a cumbersome process, and when James II succeeded his brother in February 1685 there were 'scores of surrendered charters and drafts of renewals' awaiting the great seal, Appleby's among them. On 31 July, two days after the issuing of a new charter to York, James II granted to Appleby:

> ... a fair or market for purchase and sale of all manner of goods, cattle, horses, mares, geldings, the said fair or market to begin in any year for all time at and on the second Thursday in the month of April and to last, be held and guarded for two days at any convenient place within the said liberties and precincts of the same as shall seem fit to the Mayor Aldermen and Capital Burgesses of the Common Council of the said town or to the greater number of them with all and sundry tolls, levies, viages, stallages, and other profits from the fair or market aforesaid proceeding or accruing ... Provided always we reserve for ourselves ... full power and authority from time to time and at all times hereafter to remove the Mayor, Recorder, Aldermen, Common Clerk, Coroner, Sword bearer, Serjeant at Mace and any one or more of the Aldermen and Capital Burgesses of the Common Council Chamberlain and

---

9   W. Harrison, *Description of England, 1587,* ed. G. Edelen (Washington D.C., 1994), p. 394.
10   As later reported in, e.g. *Gazette*, 5 Jun. 1819.
11   M. Holdgate, *The Story of Appleby-in-Westmorland* (Kirkby Stephen, 2006), pp. 79-160; M. Holmes, *Proud Northern Lady* (London, 1975).
12   P. D. Halliday, *Dismembering the Body Politic: Partisan Politics in England's Towns, 1650-1730* (Cambridge, 1998), pp. 191-276.

Bailiffs of the said town at the time existing at the will and pleasure of ourselves, our heirs and successors.[13]

There is no evidence that Appleby, with its established Whit Monday fair, desired one in April too: the Corporation minutes did not deign to mention the 1685 charter.[14]   Even if it had been enrolled, it would have become void in 1688 when the King demanded its return,[15] and proclaimed that all charters issued since 1679 were cancelled and would be replaced. James II's motives were obvious. In 1672 when Duke of York and heir to the throne, he had converted to his mother's Roman Catholic faith;[16] but now in 1685, having surmounted attempts to exclude him from the throne he was intent – defying 'the political truths that had made his brother's efforts so successful'[17] – on packing a parliament that would repeal the 1673 Test Acts debarring Roman Catholics from the Lords and Commons. To this end he was not only asserting his authority over boroughs but also dismissing county lord-lieutenants. Presiding over both Westmorland and Cumberland was Thomas Tufton, Earl of Thanet, owner of Appleby Castle and the dominant influence in the corporation; in 1687 he was removed from office.[18] But before James II had completed the reissue of borough charters preparatory to the election of a packed parliament, his nephew and son-in-law William of Orange, prompted by a coded invitation from seven men of influence across the political spectrum, landed in Devon in November 1688 and led his forces towards London. Seemingly aghast at the crisis he had precipitated and unwilling to precipitate civil war, James abandoned his army and fled to France; 'there is a simpleton who for a mass has lost three kingdoms', remarked Charles Maurice le Tellier, archbishop of Reims.[19] An ad hoc parliamentary assembly declared in February 1689 that he had abdicated.

There is every reason to believe that Appleby Corporation welcomed the 'Glorious Revolution' that proclaimed William III and Mary II as joint rulers: it marked the event by turning its memoranda and minutes book upside down and commencing entries at the other end; replacing with an anti-Popish oath the former requirement for office holders to abjure the Solemn League and

---

13   Kendal Archive Centre, WSMB/A/1, Charter of James II 1685, with typescript translation produced by the Corporation of Appleby (undated, unpubl.); the translation of the original Latin is accurate.

14   Kendal Archive Centre, WSMB/A/2/1, Memoranda and Minute Books of Appleby Corporation, vol. III, 1685-1729.

15   W. Hewitson, 'The Appleby Charters', *Transactions of the Cumberland & Westmorland Antiquarian and Archaeological Society*, 1st ser., [*CW1*] vol. xi (1891), pp. 279-285. Hewitson was town clerk of Appleby.

16   J. Miller, *James II* (London, 1978), p. 59.

17   Halliday, *Dismembering Body Politic*, 261.

18   Lord Macaulay, *History of England* (London, 1889, Popular Edition), vol 1, p. 483

19   Quoted in J. Childs, *The Army, James II and the Glorious Revolution* (Manchester, 1980), p.168. As to whether the 'Glorious Revolution' should be interpreted as an establishment coup or a proto-popular uprising, cf. W. Speck, *Reluctant Revolutionaries* (Oxford, 1989), S. Pincus *1688* (Yale, 2009).

Covenant; and hanging William of Orange's portrait in the mayoral parlour. The borough found itself 'an ancient corporation by prescription, without any known written charter now in force'; and so it remained.[20] As a local historian later put it, this was 'a singular state of things ... the surrenders made by the burgesses of Appleby in 1685 and 1688 were both void as never having been enrolled, and the charter of 1685 was also void, as made upon a void surrender'.[21] Not until 1885 was Appleby rescued from two centuries of legal limbo when Queen Victoria issued a new charter of incorporation, in responding to a petition from the borough in compliance with the 1882 Municipal Corporations Act.

It is most improbable that Appleby Corporation would have attempted to avail itself of a fair granted by a royal charter it had not wanted, and which had been in any case withdrawn. The only Appleby fair listed in the 1698 *English Chapman's and Traveller's Handbook* was for May 11, 12 and 13, the dates of Whitsun Eve, Whitsunday and Whit Monday.[22] No surviving edition of Ogilby's eighteenth-century *Traveller's Pocket Book* mentioned an April fair in Appleby;[23] nor did any similar publication.[24] True, Nicolson & Burn's 1777 *History of Cumberland & Westmorland* – two weighty volumes written for antiquarians, not travelling salesmen – stated that 'King James the second's fair is held on the second Thursday in April and the day following';[25] but this is probably because Richard Burn of Orton Hall, author of the Westmorland section of the *History*, derived his information simply from the contents of the 1685 charter.   No mention of the imaginary King James Fair is to be found in a range of nineteenth-century directories covering Appleby, with one exception, in which the wording indicates that the information was copied directly from Nicolson & Burn.[26]

There is indeed no evidence before the mid-twentieth century of anyone suggesting that Appleby's June fair had anything to do with this or any other charter. In 1935, raising the question of the origins of the 'New Fair', the *Herald* was content to state 'the fact that it is so ancient that no one knows when it originated'.[27] But in 1945 Alderman Richard Jackson Dawson of

20   J. Nicolson & R. Burn, *History of Westmorland and Cumberland* (London ,1777, repr. 1976), ed. B.C. Jones, vol. I, p. 317-8.

21   R.S. Ferguson, *History of Westmorland* (London, 1894), pp. 149-50.

22   *English Chapman's and Traveller's Almanack* (1698), list for 'Applesh', probably an abbreviation of 'Applebyshire', a term sometimes applied to Appleby and its surrounds.

23   Numerous issues from between 1751 and 1788, not all of them bearing a date and with inconsistent numbering of editions and listing format, are at least alike in not including an April fair for Appleby.

24   See chapter 3, notes 6 and 7 below.

25   Nicolson & Burn, *Westmorland & Cumberland*, I, p. 421.

26   W. Parson & W. White, *History, Directory and Gazetteer of Cumberland and Westmorland* (1829) p. 522; I Slater, *Royal National Commercial Directory Cumberland, Lancashire and Westmorland* (1869) p. 6; T. Bulmer, *History, Topography & Directory of Westmoreland* (1885); *Kelly's Directory of Westmorland* (1894). The exception is P.J. Mannex, *History, Topography and Directory of Westmorland* (1849), p. 124.

27   *Herald*, 15 Jun. 1935.

Appleby, a veteran of local government (Figure 6),[28] affronted by what he considered the excesses of the Fair that had followed VE Day, resolved to find a mechanism to bring it to an end and made the first reported assertion that Appleby Fair dated from 1685. Appleby's charters were kept at the Moot Hall; a former town clerk had translated them, and Dawson was presumably aware of their contents. But he speculated that there must have been another one issued in 1685 that authorised the June fair, and told his fellow councillors that 'the first thing they had to discover was the charter'.[29] However implausible the suggestion that James II had given Appleby simultaneous charters granting new fairs for different months, was there a missing document somewhere to be found in Appleby Castle? Lord Hothfield, who had served

Figure 6. Richard Jackson Dawson wearing the mayoral chain. Photograph taken by Keith Morgan from a 1930s original and reproduced by kind permission of Appleby Town Council.

as mayor for the duration of the War, undertook to search his muniment room, recalling perhaps the discovery of the original charter for Brough Hill Fair there in 1916.[30] No source suggests that he found anything more; but a myth had been born. *Country Life* stated in 1950 that Appleby Fair was 'chartered'.[31] In 1955 *The Cumberland & Westmorland Herald* told its readers that unspecified 'old local histories' attributed the Fair's origins to a charter granted by James II in 1685 and added the unhelpful rider that 'It is uncertain to who that charter was granted for no trace of it can be found today'.[32]

In 1965, when abolition was again being mooted, Michael Jopling, M.P. for Westmorland, though a professed convert to the view that 'something has got to be done', told the press that 'he had consulted the Public Records Office and could find no evidence of the existence of any charter for the fair'.[33]

28   *Observer*, 23 Apr. 1907 reports his election as Westmorland County Councillor for Long Marton. His house at Croft Ends, Brampton, adjoined the road where much of the Fair activity took place.

29   *Herald*, 15 Sep. 1945. The press report does not indicate his reasoning. He was presumably aware of the contents of the 1685 charter held by the Council (notes 13 and 15 above); he possibly imagined that James II issued a later charter changing the fair's dates.

30   D. Scott, 'Recent Discoveries in the Muniment Rooms of Appleby Castle and Skipton Castle' *CW2* XVIII (1918), pp. 189-210.

31   *Country Life*, 18 Aug. 1950, pp. 533-35.

32   *Herald*, 11 Jun. 1955.

33   *Herald*, 12 Jun. 1965.

His words had little impact; the myth had taken root. The Romani scholar Ian Hancock has shown how the fictitious claim that Gypsies had no words for 'duty', 'possession', 'truth' and 'beauty' was unquestioningly re-cycled in the nineteenth century by a succession of quasi-authoritative books.[34] The same process is evident in literature on Appleby Fair. As collections of photographs, tourist guides and websites proliferated, the 1685 charter story was routinely repeated. With appropriate embroidery, it gradually took hold among Gypsy/Travellers too. There is no reason to suppose that James II would have dissented from the attitude that led England's ruling class to enact and keep in force until 1783 the Egyptians Acts of 1530 and 1554, whereby acting or even looking like a Gypsy was potentially a capital offence;[35] but mythology transformed him into a benign sovereign granting a fair for Gypsies in a charter since lost, destroyed or concealed. Shortly before the 2012 Fair a representative of the Gypsy Council secretariat rang up Appleby Town Council requesting a copy of 'our charter', expressed puzzlement on being told that the Council did not know of the existence of any such document, and did not take up the offer of a transcript of the void charter of 1685.

The foreword to a 2011 publication on Appleby Fair shows how creatively the myth has been subverted and re-fashioned:

> Although the fair is believed by most Gypsy-Travellers to be authorised by royal charter, opponents of the fair have cast doubt on the legal status of that charter. Luckily, there is a vast area of English common law and statute concerned with the regulation of Fairs and Markets ... Even though the charter may be lost, the law presumes that it did once exist.[36]

The law makes no such presumption; and it was 'opponents of the fair' who came up with the notion that it was authorised by a charter in the first place. But the story will die hard: in both 2013 and 2014 the *Daily Mail* accompanied its bilious reports of the Fair with the information that 'King James II granted a Royal Charter allowing the horse fair to be held "near the River Eden"'.[37] This much-repeated quotation from what was in any case an invalid and irrelevant charter is also imaginary.

---

34   I. Hancock, 'Duty and Beauty, possession and truth: lexical impoverishment as control', in T. Acton & G. Mundy eds., *Romani culture and Gypsy identity*, (Hatfield, 1997), pp. 180-87.

35   Mayall, *Gypsy-Travellers in 19th C. Society* , Appendix 1, pp. 189-90.

36   Sagar-Musgrave and Lloyd, *Appleby Fair,* Introduction.

37   *Daily Mail* on-line, 11 Jun. 2013.

Chapter 4:

The Origins of Appleby Fair

If it had indeed nothing to do with James II's charter of 1685, when and how did Appleby Fair begin?[1] In 1966, when views on its origins had yet to become an article of faith, Richard Wade suggested in the *Journal of the Gypsy Lore Society* that the belief of some Travellers in a charter was mistaken.[2] Probably drawing on recent investigations by lawyers on behalf of his Gypsy/Traveller friend Silvester Gordon Boswell to support the contention that Appleby Fair had a right to its traditional Gallows Hill location,[3] Wade cited the claim in Garnet's 1912 agrarian survey of Westmorland that it could be traced back to a proclamation by the mayor of Appleby in October 1750.[4] In response to the representations of 'sevl of the inhabitants of this Borough and other Persons that it would not only greatly tend to the advantage of the Inhabitants of the Borough in general but also to the increasing the Revenue thereof', the mayor had decreed that:

> ... a Shew of Horses and Sheep and also of Black Cattle – in Case it should please God to cease the distemper among them or the ffairs and Markets to be legally opened, shall be henceforth for ever hereafter duly opened and held in Battleborough on Gallows Hill and Brownbanks within the said Borough on the first and second days of June and also on the twenty ninth and thirtieth days of September in every year except when any of those shall happen on a Sunday, then the said shall be held on the day or days following as it shall happen...[5]

Gallows Hill – now usually known as Fair Hill – was common land on the margins between Appleby and the village of Brampton; Battlebarrow (as it is now spelled) is the road leading to it from the Sands (Figure 7). However, the specified dates do not correspond with any subsequently recorded fair at Appleby, and the Corporation minutes make no further reference to this

1   The case made out in chapters 3 and 4 of this book is summarised in A. Connell, 'When and how did Appleby Fair begin?', *CW3*(2014), pp. 309-11.

2   R.A.R. Wade, 'The Saving of Appleby Fair', *Journal of the Gypsy Lore Society*, XLV (1966), pp. 29-37.

3   Kendal Archive Centre, WSRDNW 3/1 Box 6, Correspondence on Appleby Fair: letter with enclosures from S.G.Boswell of Spalding, Lincs., to the Clerk of North Westmorland Rural District Council, 14 Aug. 1965. For Wade's close association with Boswell, see chapter 10.

4   J.W. Garnet, *Westmorland Agriculture* (London, 1912), pp. 114-117. The same view is advanced in Holdgate, *Story of Appleby*, p. 170.

5   Kendal Archive Centre, WSMB/A/2/1, Appleby Borough Corporation Minutes, vol IV, 1729-1764, 26 Oct. 1750. 'Black cattle' was a term commonly applied to cattle from Scotland.

'Shew'. There is no evidence that the intention that it be 'duly advertised in the Papers … and printed Advertisements dispersed through the Kingdom at the Expense of this Borough' was carried out. It was not included in the *Traveller's Pocket Book*, the 1761 edition of which listed for Appleby : 'A fair on Whitsun Eve for horned cattle, on Whitsun Monday for linen cloth and merchandise, on 10 August – the patronal day of St Lawrence, to whom Appleby parish church was dedicated – for horses, sheep, and linen cloth' (See Appendix 4)[6]. The *Universal Magazine* of 1761 listed the same information.[7]

If nothing came of the 1750 mayoral proclamation, why not? The explanation may lie in the endemic political tension in Appleby between the Tuftons, the dominant landowning force in the Eden Valley, and the Lowthers, the greatest property-owners in Cumberland and Westmorland. Membership of the corporation and parliamentary representation of the borough were likewise divided between adherents of the two sides; sometimes the spoils were shared by agreement, sometimes fiercely contested. The town clerk for 1750-51 who wrote out the resolution to hold a fair on Gallows Hill was John Robinson, Lowther agent and man of business (Figure 8);[8] the mayor, James Parkin, was also a Lowther client. They may have been venturing a political gambit rather than making a serious proposal. The Earl of Thanet owned the largest share of rights to the Gallows Hill common, and took the view that it was outside the borough boundary; the mayor's proclamation challenged him. Further provocation was apparent in the proposal that the second new fair should take place on the last two days of September, thereby pre-empting Brough Hill Fair, which took place on Thanet's land. When Tufton supporters resumed the mayoralty and clerkship in 1751, Parkin's proclamation passed into oblivion. Instead the newly-acceded 21 year-old eighth Earl of Thanet took the offensive (Figure 9); in 1754 he tried the strength of the even younger heir to the Lowther estates, Sir James Lowther, by attempting to secure the election of both Appleby members in the general election, an enterprise in which he ultimately failed at enormous expense to both sides.[9]

Twenty years later there was another round of hostilities. In April 1774, when both the mayor and town clerk were related to John Robinson,[10] the corporation resolved that it would lay its claim to Gallows Hill before the parliamentary enclosure commissioners, and if the claim were disallowed would take immediate steps 'to support and maintain the rights and privileges

---

6   Ogilby, *Pocket Book*, 2nd ed. (1761), p. 270.
7   *Universal Magazine*, Sep. 1761, p. 113.
8   A. Connell, 'Appleby in Westminster: John Robinson, MP', *CW3*, X (2010), pp. 217-236.
9   B. Bonsall, *Sir James Lowther and Cumberland and Westmorland Elections 1754-1776* (Manchester, 1960), pp. 17-34.
10   Joseph Deane, the mayor, was a cousin; Joseph Robinson, the town clerk, a brother.

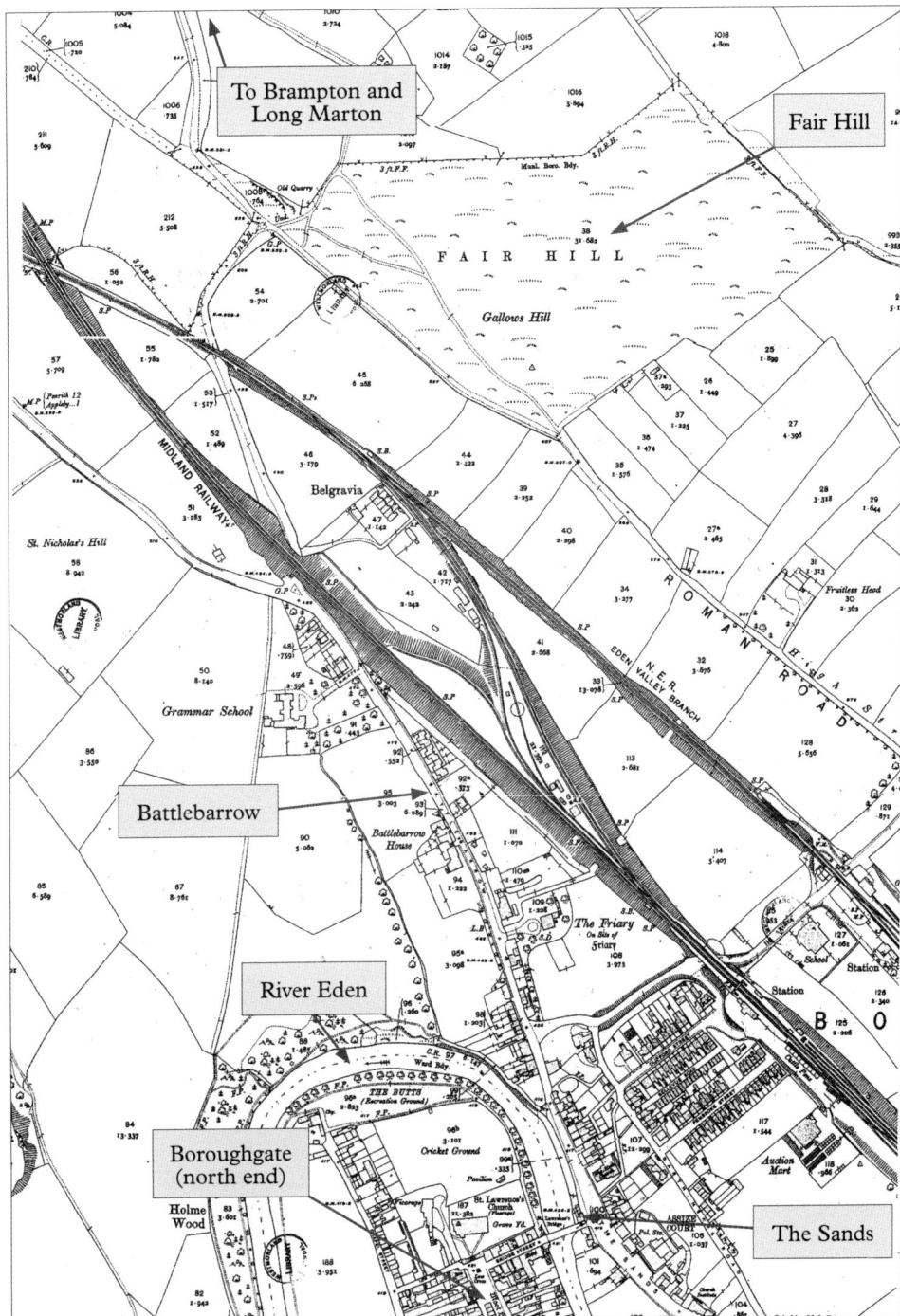

Figure 7. From the Ordnance Survey Map of 1915, showing Fair Hill, the River Eden and the centre of Appleby. Reproduced by kind permission of the Local Studies section of the Kendal branch of Cumbria County Library.

Figure 8. John Robinson (1727-1802),
town clerk of Appleby 1750-51, mayor
1760-61. Photograph by Keith Morgan
from the painting by G.F. Joseph.
Reproduced by kind permission of
Appleby Town Council.

Figure 9. Sackville Tufton, eighth Earl of
Thanet, as a young man. Artist unknown;
photograph by John Tillotson. Reproduced by
kind permission of the owner.

of the Borough'.[11] In 1775 in the *Newcastle Chronicle* of 3 June the Borough
and Corporation of Appleby gave notice of a 'Shew of Cattle, Horses and
Sheep' to be 'annually held on ... Gallows-Hill within the Borough and
Corporation aforesaid'; it would take place on Wednesday 14 June and on the
second Wednesday of June each year thereafter.[12] That this 'Shew' actually
took place is confirmed by a report of 22 June in the *Cumberland Pacquet,*
published in Whitehaven:

> We hear from Appleby that at the new Fair, held nigh that town on
> Wednesday se'en night, there were upwards of 20,000 sheep which
> sold well; cattle a good deal lower than they had done and hams pretty
> reasonable. – It is supposed a much greater number of buyers would
> have attended, had it been more generally known; numbers of people
> having only accidental information of the day it was held on.[13]

In June 1776 the corporation repeated the advertisement of the previous
year, but provoked a tart response from Thanet:

> The Words (within the Borough and Corporation of Appleby) have been
> falsely inserted, with an artful Design that the same may be produced

---

11   Appleby B C Minutes, Vol V, 1764-1795
12   *Newcastle Chronicle*, 3 Jun. 1775
13   *Cumberland Pacquet*, 22 Jun. 1775

at some future Time as Evidence of a Right which never existed, to the Prejudice of the Owners ... Notice is hereby given that the aforesaid Parcel of Ground is a considerable Distance from the said Borough and Corporation of Appleby ... and is the Property of the Right Honourable Sackville, Earl of Thanet ... and several other Persons ... who, for the Convenience of the Public, have permitted their Shares to lie open; that a Shew of Cattle, Horses and Sheep might be holden thereon.[14]

We may surmise that Appleby Corporation's 1774 resolution to lay claim to Gallows Hill had been made in reaction to it becoming known that Thanet, simultaneously promoting both the fortunes of his numerous tenant farmers and his own local pre-eminence, would facilitate a livestock fair there in June. Such a development, on the town's doorstep but beyond the reach of its tolls and likely to undercut the old-established Whit fair, could hardly go unchallenged. Whether or not the new fair took place in that year, it certainly did in 1775, when the Corporation, having presumably got nowhere with the enclosure commissioners, asserted not by virtue of any charter, but on the grounds that it was located within the borough, its ownership of an occasion it could not prevent. Thanet of course rejected the claim, and the subsequent silence of the Corporation's minutes book suggests it was swiftly abandoned. Although Sir James Lowther, created Earl of Lonsdale in 1784, was, with as many as eight MPs at his behest, a far more significant, if erratic, figure in parliamentary politics, the Tuftons were regaining local primacy, particularly after John Robinson, now an MP and government minister, broke with the Lowthers and in 1781 sold his Appleby burgages to Thanet.[15]

There is adequate evidence to be confident that by then the new fair in June was an established event. Nicolson's and Burn's 1777 antiquarian survey of Westmorland did not mention it in the context of either Appleby or Brampton, but since it went to press in 1775, this is not surprising.[16] In 1781 the *Cumberland Pacquet* reported that there had been 'near 40,000' sheep on show, and on the Wednesday more cattle 'than for many years past'.[17] There was a similar report in 1783: 'We are informed from Appleby that on Wednesday last the new fair for cattle was very brisk. A prodigious number were brought to market, and most of them sold at high prices'.[18] In 1784 'sheep and horses sold very high, but milk cows were lower than of late; however cloth sold well. The whole was a good fair'.[19] Although the *Pacquet*, published in Whitehaven some fifty miles from Appleby, thereafter ceased

---

14   *Newcastle Chronicle*, 22 Jun. 1776
15   Connell, 'Appleby in Westminster', *CW3* (2010)
16   Nicolson & Burn, p. 321; introduction, p. xxi. More than a year passed between Burn's copy going to press and the book's publication.
17   *Cumberland Pacquet*, 26 Jun. 1781.
18   Ibid., 17 Jun. 1783 (fair on 11 June).
19   Ibid., 22 Jun. 1784 (fair on 9 June).

to report the Fair, its inclusion in contemporary editions of Ogilby, Owen's *New Book of Fairs* and Bowles's *Post Chaise Companion* indicates that it was ongoing.[20] They concur, however, in listing it for cattle and sheep, without mention of horses, and as fixed on 10 June, not the second Wednesday in the month. This may indicate a temporary change in arrangements; or it may be a copied error in publications whose selling point should have been their accuracy. The next surviving press reports are from the second decade of the nineteenth century; and they are quite clear that the main day of the Fair was 'Wednesday last'.[21]

20   Ogilby, 22nd edn. (1782), 23rd edn. (1788), 24th edn. (1794). M. Owen, *New Book of Fairs*, MDCCLXXX, MDCCLXXXVIII, MDCCXCIX. C. Bowles, *Post Chaise Companion*, 1794, vol II.
21   *Westmorland Advertiser*, 13 Jun. 1812, 14 Jun. 1817, 12 Jun. 1819 etc. The paper was published on Saturdays.

Chapter 5:

Evolution: the Drovers' Fair

The economic driver of Appleby New Fair seems to have been the burgeoning traffic in livestock reared in Scotland. The elimination of traditional Border banditry, the ban on Irish cattle imports after 1667 and the ending of customs duties following the 1707 Act of Union all encouraged greater movement of 'Scotch-reared' cattle and sheep into England. As Peter Roebuck has demonstrated, droving was of increasing importance to Cumbrian agriculture. Drovers were charged well above the normal rate for temporary grazing stances, and local farmers had the first pick in purchasing itinerant stock for overwintering and sale in the subsequent season.[1] Around 15,000 Scotch cattle passed through the Musgrave estate at Edenhall alone as early as 1712; and recently discovered records suggest that a similar number, and possibly more, travelled through other parts of the estate in the same year. 'This was big business indeed':[2] the suggested figure of 80,000 for the annual totality of Scotch cattle crossing the border by 1750 now seems far too low.[3] Two droving routes from Scotland converged on Appleby.[4] There were obvious advantages in moving sheep and cattle long distances when the nights were shortest; and with the established livestock fairs, at Carlisle thirty miles north and Brough ten miles south, in late August and September respectively,[5] the June fair established in 1775 met a demand, more especially since New Fair patrons, although they might eat, drink and dance in the town less than a mile from the fairground, paid no dues to the Corporation— unlike those who traded at Appleby's Whitsuntide fair.

Suggestive evidence comes from the ledger of George and Matthew Atkinson, recording transactions between 1779 and 1790.[6] Their home village of Temple Sowerby lay on the road from Penrith to Appleby, and the Atkinsons had an old-established tanning business. Probably assisted by their younger brother Richard, who had gone to London and was making

---

1   P. Roebuck, 'Cattle-droving through Cumbria after the Union: the Stances on the Musgrave estate, 1707-12, *CW3* (2012), pp. 143-158.

2   Idem, 'Cattle-droving through Cumbria, 1707-12: New Evidence from the Musgrave Estate, *CW3* (2013), pp. 256-60.

3   A.R.B. Haldane, *The Drove Roads of Scotland* (Newton Abbot, 1973), p. 178.

4   K.J. Bonser, *The Drovers* (London, 1970), pp. 150-1.

5   There was an old-established Whitsuntide fair at Rosley Hill, near Wigton. It primarily served westbound droving routes; but when Whit fell in May some of the stock purchased there is likely to have been walked south-east and sold on at Gallows Hill.

6   The Atkinson Ledger is in the possession of Richard M.C. Atkinson, a descendant of George who is currently working on the family history, and has been accessed by his kind permission.

his fortune in international commerce, and by John Robinson, Treasury Secretary from 1770 to 1782,[7] George and Matthew were able to establish themselves as country bankers in the 1770s. Their customers included drovers, who handled large sums of cash to pay for stances en route to selling their stock, either to local farmers or to other drovers who would take it further south. During the 1780s, the Atkinson 'Drovers Accounts' turned over some £30,000 annually, with profits of up to 10 per cent,[8] some of it doubtless derived from dealing done at the new fair near Appleby. Evidence for its operation during the war years, 1793-1815, is scant, but there is no reason to doubt an unbroken annual sequence. Press attention became more regular following the establishment in Kendal of weekly newspapers for Westmorland in the second decade of the nineteenth century. The Tory *Gazette* and the Whig *Mercury* carried reports on what they usually called Brampton Hill, less often Appleby, New Fair.[9] The papers' mutual antipathy notwithstanding, their reports, conveyed to Kendal along twenty-four miles of winding road that crossed two moors and a steep gorge, tended to be similar in tone. In 1812 'cattle of all kinds were sold dear' and 'Scotch sheep fetched high prices' as did horses, though 'there were few … all of an inferior sort'.[10] In 1818:

> The annual Fair called Appleby and Brampton New Fair, held on Wednesday last, was attended by the greatest number of visitors ever known. Cattle, Sheep and Horses, of which there were immense numbers, sold at high prices, which were not a little enhanced by the luxuriant appearance of the country, and the uncommon fine weather. This Fair has become of late years of considerable note, and we doubt not will in a little time be the means of additional improvements to the mercantile and farming interests of that part of the country.[11]

The 1823 fair was 'well attended, and the sale in general very brisk. Sheep experienced an advance in price; good horses and ponies suitable for the saddle were in great demand … Black cattle and milch cows fetched improved prices'.[12] Parson and White's 1829 Directory esteemed Appleby's June fair as 'nearly equal in consequence to the great fair held on Brough Hill'.[13] A modern assessment is that for horses it was on a par with the fairs at Howden,

---

7   A. Connell, 'John Robinson (1727-1802), Richard Atkinson (1739-85), Government, Commerce and Politics in the Age of the American Revolution: 'From the North', *Northern History*, L.1 (Mar 2013), pp. 54-76.

8   Atkinson Ledger, pp. 16, 57, 88, 138, 173.

9   The *Westmorland Gazette*, founded in 1818, retains its name; the now-defunct *Kendal Mercury* began life in 1812 as the *Westmorland Advertiser and Kendal Chronicle*.

10   *Westmorland Advertiser*, 13 Jun. 1812.

11   *Gazette*, 10 Jun. 1818.

12   *Advertiser*, 14 Jun. 1823.

13   W. Parson & W. White, *History, Directory and Gazetteer of Cumberland and Westmorland* (Leeds, 1829, repr. Beckermet, 1976), p. 522.

Horncastle and Lincoln as 'the chief outlets for the hunters, hackneys and light draught-horses much in demand'.[14] In 1840 the *Gazette* reported that Brampton Fair was 'considered by those who are in the regular habit of attending fairs to be the largest and best in the north of England for stock of all descriptions',[15] and was now extending over three days. Tuesday was the day for sheep dealing, when 'the hill was literally an entire mass of fleecy animals';[16] Wednesday, 'the all important day', was for cattle and horses. Thursday saw residual trading mainly in horses, with much 'swapping',[17] along with peripheral dealing in 'cloth, cotton and other goods'.[18]

A municipal attempt to lure away some of this business is evident from the announcement in May 1836, that, 'in compliance with a Requisition presented to the Mayor of Appleby by a numerous and respectable body of Wool Growers', there would be toll-free fairs for the sale of wool in Appleby on Wednesdays 15 June and 27 July.[19] The press reported a 'pretty good show of Cheviot and Leicester wool' and 'a number of buyers from different parts', but they proved reluctant to buy.[20] In 1837 'Appleby Wool Fair' was advertised as an established event, but the lack of any mention of it thereafter suggests that it failed to compete with the fair on the hill.[21] The fall in the annual sum for which the Corporation could farm out Metley and Gatley tolls from £102 in 1838 to £90 in 1842 indicates dwindling trade in the town,[22] and perhaps explains the launch of an 'Appleby Horse Fair' in February 1843. A year later:

> The fair was held on Saturday last in the market place. The show of horses was very indifferent, and chiefly consisted of draught horses. Buyers were extremely scarce – indeed we only heard of a single horse being sold, and the prices were on average lower than last year. A great many farmers attended but principally to observe the state of the fair. This is the second and one will be held annually about this time of the year ... on account of the depressed state of the markets, we were not at all surprised by the dull sale experienced.[23]

In 1845, the same event, described as 'usually' taking place 'on the Monday following old Candlemas Day',[24] saw 'a very scanty show of horses'; in 1846

14   B.A. Holderness in *Agrarian History of England & Wales* Vol. IV, 1750-1850 ed. G.E. Mingay, (Cambridge, 1989), p. 89.
15   *Gazette*, 13 Jun. 1840.
16   *Mercury* 12 Jun. 1847.
17   *Mercury* 14 Jun. 1845.
18   *Gazette*, 17 Jun. 1820.
19   *Mercury*, 4 Jun. 1836.
20   *Gazette*, 18 Jun. 1836.
21   *Mercury*, 17 Jun. 1837.
22   Appleby B C Minutes, vol. IX, 1836-`1862, 15 Oct. 1838, 10 Oct. 1842.
23   *Mercury*, 24 Feb. 1844.
24   *Mercury*, 22 Feb. 1845.

it took place on a Tuesday, with the same outcome,[25] after which it too passed into oblivion.

Meanwhile the 'New Fair' on Brampton Hill was routinely described in the Kendal press as a 'very extensive and important fair'[26] that was 'resorted to by dealers and graziers from all parts of Great Britain and Ireland.'[27] Reports focused on livestock prices, emphasising that it was more an occasion for 'business transactions' than for 'pleasure seekers'.[28] They offer only the occasional hint of the dust or mud of the hill, the bleating, lowing and whinnying, the cries of vendors, the crowded lanes and highways, the overflowing Appleby inns and lodging houses, the drinking and the dancing through the short nights. In 1820, a downpour on the Wednesday evening 'compelled the major part of the crowd to seek for shelter in the town of Appleby, where dancing was commenced and continued until a late hour'.[29] There is no suggestion of a controlling organisation; the Fair happened and any entertainment was al fresco, as when 'a Belt was given by the young gentlemen of Appleby school to be wrestled for ... amongst the rousing acclamations of hundreds of people'.[30]

Like passers of counterfeit money, pickpockets were a hazard, though Westmorland newspaper readers might have taken comfort that the 'light-fingered gentry' were not local villains: they probably came from Leeds,[31] and 'their success was small, as the magistrates and constabulary have of late years been the means of preventing in great measure these marauders from enjoying the benefits of their nefarious practices'.[32] The *Mercury* warned in 1847 of 'An Old Dodge', carried out by gangs of three 'sharpers'.[33] Sharper A approaches a farmer and offers to buy sheep or cattle from him. As they negotiate, B passes by leading a horse and A breaks off to make B a handsome offer for it. He produces money, but before the deal is sealed C appears and orders B to leave because 'the master' has a grievance against A and will not allow one of his horses to be sold to him. B leads the horse away, whereupon A asks the farmer to go after B and purchase the horse, which A will immediately buy from him. The farmer obliges, but finds when he returns that A has vanished, leaving him with an over-priced horse and his own stock unsold. In 1851 the *Mercury* lamented that despite its warnings there were still those at the fair 'so ignorant and simple' as to fall for the 'Horse Trick', citing an unfortunate from Lanarkshire, 'duped out of £41,

25   *Mercury,* 21 Feb. 1846.
26   *Mercury,* 12 Jun. 1847.
27   *Mercury,* 17 Jun. 1848.
28   *Gazette,* 14 Jun. 1851.
29   *Gazette,* 17 Jun. 1820.
30   *Gazette,* 12 Jun. 1824.
31   *Gazette,* 16 Jun. 1849.
32   *Gazette,* 17 Jun. 1843.
33   *Mercury,* 12 Jun. 1847.

nearly his all'.[34]

Violence at the fair, if any, did not attract press comment; but in 1859 'towards the evening navvies and Irishmen seemed to have attained full possession of the fair, and rows and fights might be computed by the dozen'.[35] The construction of the Eden Valley Railway through Appleby had begun late in 1858.[36] The opening of the railway in 1862 on the Saturday before the Fair had an instant impact: 'an immense number of traders and excursionists availed themselves of the cheapest and most accessible mode of conveyance to one of the greatest fairs in the North of England'.[37] At the Fair's end, 'Special engines kept plying from Appleby to Clifton and Kirkby Stephen for the accommodation of the public and an immense quantity of trucks were provided at the stations for receiving cattle, sheep etc'.[38] The single track of the North Eastern railway linked Appleby with Penrith and Darlington; and from 1876 the double-track Midland line opened the way to and from Carlisle and Leeds. Trains brought many more visitors to the New Fair, who found more than livestock on offer to divert them; in 1880 'there were as usual, some shooting galleries, shows, roundabouts & c. for the delectation of youngsters'.[39]

34   *Mercury,* 15 Jun. 1850.
35   *Mercury,* 11 Jun. 1859.
36   P. Walton, *Stainmore and Eden Valley Railways* (Yeovil, 1992), pp. 76-77
37   *Mercury,* 14 Jun. 1862.
38   *Gazette,* 14 Jun. 1862
39   *Penrith Observer,* 15 Jun. 1880.

Chapter 6:

Evolution: the Horse Fair

By the last two decades of the nineteenth century what was generally designated 'Appleby New Fair' was changing, as it became clear that the railway spelled the end of droving. Permanent sale areas at stations reflected and encouraged the transportation of sheep and cattle by railway wagon: there were fortnightly sales in 'the capacious Auction Mart, adjoining the Midland Station'.[1] But auctions held to coincide with the Fair provided only a temporary symbiosis between old and new. There were now three Penrith weekly newspapers reporting on it – the Liberal *Herald,* the Conservative *Observer* and the Methodist *Advertiser*; all concurred in the view that 'the "glory" of this fair for the sale of cattle and sheep would appear to have departed'.[2] Appleby New Fair gradually became 'confined to the exhibition and sale of horses of every description, for which it is one of the best markets in the kingdom'.[3] The trade in cattle and sheep had a lingering half-life: in 1893 there was 'an unusually large number of cattle', though 'only a light show of sheep';[4] in 1898, 'the supply of sheep and cattle was smaller than usual';[5] in 1903 there were 'absolutely no cattle on Gallows Hill'.[6]

Droving had passed into history by the dawn of the twentieth century,[7] but horses, often uneasy rail travellers, were still walked in small groups along the roads to Appleby, to be put through their paces on the Sands, washed in the Eden, and then purchased on the spot or taken up to Gallows Hill for sale. In 1888 the *Herald* reported that 'the heaviest feature of the fair … is the horse trade, which commences on the "Sands" near Appleby Bridge'. Opinions among horse dealers differed as to whether prices were better on Tuesdays or Wednesdays. 'Be this as it may, a good turn out always takes place on the Sands'.[8] In 1894 'the display of horses was one of the largest on record. Good animals, suitable for field, road, or harness, were the class in most request, and commanded really good prices. Dealers were present from all parts of the kingdom, and included several buyers from tramway companies'.[9] In 1898, 'hackneys and roadsters were a smart lot, but only the

1   T.F. Bulmer, *History, Topography and Directory of Westmorland* (Preston, 1885), p. 116.
2   *Herald,* 17 Jun. 1882.
3   *Penrith Advertiser,* 10 Jun 1890.
4   *Herald,* 17 Jun. 1893.
5   *Herald,* 11 Jun. 1898.
6   *Herald,* 13 June 1903.
7   Bonser, *Drovers,* pp. 224-229.
8   *Herald,* 16 Jun. 1888.
9   *Herald,* 16 Jun. 1894.

picked animals were sold at anything like satisfactory rates, and these were understood to be largely for military purposes'.[10] In 1901, with the market distorted by the shipping out of hundreds of thousands of cavalry and draught horses for British forces fighting the Boers in South Africa, 'big prices were asked for all classes, and good trade was done', not only with 'hard-headed Westmorland farmers' (Figure 10). The *Herald* reported:

> Good agricultural horses were bought from £50 to £70, and in some cases up to £80; lighter cart horses changed hands at from £30 to £40; hackneys and harness horses made from £30 to £50, and ponies £15 to £35. Government agents were present who purchased horses as cavalry remounts for the depot at York at prices ranging up to £40.[11]

By this time the common land that was the centrepiece of the Fair was unequivocally within the boundaries of Appleby. The town had lost its parliamentary borough status in 1832, and the corporation ceased to be the battleground of competing aristocratic interests. The Lowthers were unquestionably the dominant political force in Westmorland as a whole, but in the microcosm of Appleby and its surrounds, the Tuftons called most of the shots. Sir Henry Tufton, recently ennobled as Lord Hothfield, far from objecting to the inclusion of Gallows Hill within Bongate Ward of the

Figure 10. Street scene in front of Appleby Shire Hall, during the Fair. Date unknown, but probably c. 1900. Photographer unknown. Reproduced by kind permission of Appleby-in-Westmorland Society.

10   *Herald*, 11 Jun. 1898.
11   *Herald*, 15 Jun. 1901.

municipal borough of Appleby, as defined by the Victorian charter of 1885, probably facilitated it.[12]   The Liberal majority in the reconstituted Council reflected his political leanings; and when he switched to the Conservatives in the 1890s, the balance on the Borough Council shifted with him.[13] But what had Appleby Council to do with fairs?   In 1885 the traditional Whitsuntide event, 'long fallen into desuetude' with 'no stock of any description' on show, had been paraded by the Mayor and Council for the last time.[14] That left St Lawrence's Fair in mid-August;[15] and on the second Wednesday in June the New Fair, which – on the evidence of both minute books and press reports – Appleby's civic leaders would studiously ignore for another sixty years. Its temporary effect on the life of the town was nonetheless undeniable, as the log books of Appleby's elementary schools demonstrate.   In 1863, when the New Fair fell in the week following Whitsuntide, the National School in Bongate closed for a week.   More usually, closure was restricted to Tuesday and Wednesday, but attendances on the Monday and Thursday were poor.[16] In 1866 the British School in Chapel Street, closer to the sights and sounds of the Fair, remained open even on the climactic Wednesday, but numbers attending were so low that it too began routine closure.   On the Tuesday of the 1876 Fair the headmaster reported: 'Dismissed children early on account of the dangerous state of the streets caused by show of horses. Gave holiday for to-morrow, it being "New Fair" day'.[17]   In 1890, 'At the close of this morning's school we gave holiday till Thursday, owing to the "Fair", which renders the streets so dangerous that many parents will not send their little ones out'.   He was no happier ten years later, when he noted, 'These broken weeks are anything but conducive to good work being done'.[18]

That the Appleby New Fair was not considered a tourist attraction can be inferred from the first guidebook to the town, written with visitors in mind by Canon W. A. Mathews, vicar of St Lawrence's. He referred explicitly to Brough Hill Fair, 'supposed by some to have been instituted as early as the Roman occupation', but confined mention of Appleby New Fair to the information that Fair Hill took its name 'from the annual fairs held there' (Figure 11).[19] Yet the canon, as manager of St Lawrence's School for Infants and Girls, was well aware of the local impact of the Fair. In 1890, the year in which his town guide was published, he visited the school during Fair Week,

---

12   Kendal Archive Centre, WSMB/A/1, Charter of 48 Victoria 1885. Tufton was then a prominent Liberal; Gladstone was Prime Minister.
13   A. Connell, 'The Domination of Lowtherism and Toryism in Westmorland Parliamentary Elections, 1818-1895', *Northern History*, XLV.2 (2008), pp. 295-321.
14   *Observer*, 3 Jun. 1885.
15   See Appendix 4.
16   Kendal Archive Centre, WDS 71/1/1 Appleby National School Log Book, 1863-1910.
17   Kendal Archive Centre, WDS 71/2/1 Diary or Log Book of Appleby British School, 1863-1882.
18   Ibid., WDS 71/2/2, 1882-1910, entries for 10 June 1890, 11 June 1900.
19   Canon W. A. Mathews, *Guide Book to Appleby in Westmorland and its Vicinity* (Appleby, 1890), pp.43,52.

Figure 11. Roman Road and Fair Hill during Appleby Fair. Date unknown, but probably c. 1910. Photographer unknown. Reproduced by kind permission of Appleby-in-Westmorland Society.

when the log book recorded that 'during the stir a day & a half holiday was given. A good many absent for the week ... every class this & not good to work'.[20] St Lawrence's School would continue to close for the Fair during the remaining seventy years of its existence. The other two elementary schools ceased to function in 1910 following the building of a county council school in Appleby. Sited on the other side of town, between the two railway stations, the new school followed its predecessors in suspending activities at the height of the Fair. In 1913 the headmaster, William Harris, noted on the afternoon of Monday 9 June that 'owing to the dangerous character of the streets and roads during "The Fair" the school will not meet tomorrow and Wednesday'. On Friday 13 June he recorded that attendance throughout the week had 'suffered considerably'.[21]

By then the Borough Council had indirectly involved itself with the Fair, even though it did not speak its name. In January 1911 it unanimously resolved 'to consider and report upon the feasibility of acquiring the unenclosed land known as Gallows Hill for a recreation ground for the benefit of the inhabitants of the Borough in commemoration of the forthcoming Coronation of His Majesty King George V'.[22] The smoothness with which the process was carried through suggests that the decision had been prompted, if not dictated, by Appleby's two leading landowners and therefore holders

---

20   Kendal Archive Centre, WDS/71/3/1, Log Book of St. Lawrence School, Appleby, 1872-1913, week ending 13 Jun. 1890.

21   Kendal Archive Centre, WDS 71/4/1, Log Book of Appleby Council School 1910-1936, 9 Jun. 1913.

22   Appleby Borough Corporation's Minutes (1908-11), p. 138, 18 Jan. 1911.

of common rights, Henry Tufton, first Baron Hothfield and Hugh Lowther, fifth Earl of Lonsdale;[23] and 'when the two Lords agreed to the enclosure of their portions the others did the same'.[24] On 31 December 1911, with the authority of the seals and signatures of the Earl of Lonsdale, Baron Hothfield and eight others, the land was conveyed 'without consideration' to the Borough, according to section 7 of the 1906 Open Spaces Act, which allowed land to be given to local authorities so that it could be 'preserved as an open space for the enjoyment of the public'.[25]

The terms were not defined and no conditions were placed on the new owners. The Mayor had already publicly stated that the land would be enclosed 'for recreation purposes, but eventually as a money making concern', with 'every prospect of the scheme being a source of profit'.[26] Within six months the Council had accepted a tender for the enclosure of Gallows Hill and had empowered a sub-committee to 'let the herbage'.[27] In August 1912 a half-year tenancy, running from August to February, was entered into with an adjoining farm for a modest £5; Lord Hothfield then demanded and received from the Council keys to each of the two gates in the new fence.[28] In 1913 by agreement with various adjoining landowners, a water pipe was laid;[29] and by 1918 the let was from April to April, at a rental of £31.[30]

Although this sum would dwindle as the inter-war agricultural depression took hold, the agricultural tenancy was firmly established; later tenants would combine stock-grazing with the maintenance of a town rubbish tip,[31] while the Corporation did some quarrying.[32] There is no evidence that any of this was seen to be incompatible with the enjoyment of the public and little evidence as to the extent to which it was actually used for recreation: in the loop of the River Eden there was much more centrally situated green space where local children could play. Council minutes had by the 1930s ceased to make even occasional references to Gallows Hill as the 'Recreation Ground', and it was never so described by the press. However, a tenancy agreement of 1945 reaffirmed 'the right of the public to have access to the land' for 'lawful

23   Kendal Archive Centre, Borough of Appleby Letters Book (1907-11), pp.78, 82, letters of 22 and 25 Nov. 1911.

24   *Herald,* 21 Jun. 1969, letter from J.F. Whitehead to the editor.

25   The 1911 conveyance and the 1913 enclosure agreement are held by Appleby Town Council's solicitors.

26   *Herald,* 11 Nov. 1912. The occasion was the annual mayoral banquet; the Mayor was responding to toast to himself by Lord Hothfield.

27   *Herald,* 15 Jun. 1912.

28   Kendal Archive Centre, Hothfield Box 36, File 177, letter from R. Barrett, Steward of Skipton castle to W. Hewitson, Town Clerk of Appleby, 14 Nov 1912. Borough of Appleby Letters Book 1911-15, p. 396, Letter from Hewitson to Barrett.

29   Appleby BC Minutes, vol. 4, p. 279, 4 Nov. 1913.

30   Appleby BC Committee Minutes, 1914-19, p. 238, General Purposes Committee, 7 May 1918.

31   Appleby BC Minutes, vol. 6, p. 140, 21 Apr. 1926; vol. 7, p. 247, 15 Apr. 1936.

32   Appleby BC Committee Minutes, 1924-29, p. 11, Health, Highways, Property & Allotments Sub-Committee,, 7 Dec 1924.

purposes of recreation', as well as 'the right of persons resorting to the June Fair with cattle for sale to exhibit such cattle ... in accordance with custom'.[33]

At first glance the latter commitment seems inconsistent both with anecdotal recollections of the Fair being excluded from the Hill, and with the Borough Corporation's minute of 1946 asserting 'none usage of the Fair Hill for thirty five years'.[34] The answer may lie in its being defined as a cattle fair – something it had already ceased to be in 1911; future provision for it in the tenancy agreement was therefore meaningless. The readiness of Lords Hothfield and Lonsdale to part with land that was effectively their property may have had less to do with a new-found enthusiasm for public rights of access and recreation provided for by the legislation of a Liberal government that they both disliked and actively opposed,[35] than with a desire to wash their hands of the Fair. It was of no further economic importance to them, since their many tenant farmers no longer sold sheep and cattle there; and it may well have become an embarrassment for other reasons. One of the eight 'others' who signed and sealed the 1911 conveyance was William Hewitson, the veteran Town Clerk; another was Alderman Alex Heelis, and two of the remaining six were his sisters Blanche and May. The Heelis family had enjoyed a close relationship with the Tuftons for three centuries.[36]

There is little doubt that some members at least of Appleby Corporation understood that the underlying reason why it found itself the owner of Gallows Hill had not been stated in the conveyance. James F. Whitehead, then in his late teens, son of a former mayor and himself a future mayor and local historian, would recall nearly sixty years later that although the land was conveyed as a recreation ground 'this use for the newly-acquired open space did not work out for obvious reasons'; he evidently felt it unnecessary to explain what these reasons were.[37] To be sure, at a meeting of Appleby Borough Council in September 1911, the Mayor made a point of commending the way Lord Hothfield had 'helped in trying to get a recreation ground for the children'. But this was in the context of a heated discussion of the Baron's expressed wish to enclose a portion of Scattergate Green, which lay just outside the walls of Appleby Castle and was a popular play area; another councillor had

33   Tenancy agreement of 17 Jan. 1945 between the Corporation of Appleby and John B. and James N. Winter, held by Appleby Town Council's solicitors.

34   Appleby BC Committee Minutes, 1945-49, p. 113, Health & Highways, 2 Dec 1946.

35   Lonsdale's seat at Lowther Castle was the beating heart of Cumbrian Toryism. He had been active in his support for the defeated Conservative candidate for the Appleby (North Westmorland) constituency in the January 1906 General Election, and was a Conservative member of Rutland County Council. Hothfield, an unsuccessful Liberal candidate in 1880, had become a Conservative in 1895, and by 1911 was one of the extreme 'Ditchers' resisting Liberal reform of the powers of the House of Lords. A. Connell, 'Blue Sky over North Westmorland: Appleby's Liberal Decade', *CW3* (2006), pp. 195-215.

36   J. Heelis, *The Tale of Mrs William Heelis: Beatrix Potter* (Stroud, 2003). There is a fuller unpublished account of the family history by the same author in Kendal Archive Centre.

37   *Herald,* 21 Jun. 1969.

just deplored the 'green being taken from the children' by Lord Hothfield for no apparent financial reason.[38] Press reports suggest that in 1912 the New Fair took place in its usual location, with 'a very large attendance of farmers and dealers', notwithstanding torrential rain and hail on the Tuesday evening, when 'the "campers" in their flimsily constructed homes on the hill ... were nearly drowned like rats in a trap';[39] but by the following year the enclosure of Gallows Hill had been legally ratified.[40] Although the report of the 1913 Fair in the *Herald* described tents and caravans lining the roads but 'all the business' done on the Hill, this may, as in later reports, have meant not the actual open space but the Roman Road running parallel to its western fence. The locking of the gates would explain the comment that there was 'a shortage of space for a horse fair ... and it is wonderful that people are not hurt'.[41]

It is apparent both from school log books and brief press reports that the New Fair continued throughout the 1914-18 War. Such was the scale of military demand for horses in 1915 that those arriving by rail were 'picked up at highly remunerative prices at the station'.[42] In 1916, when 'hundreds of horses of all descriptions' were sold, 'the gathering was held on Tuesday and Wednesday, the scene of the former day's business being the Sands in the town, while on Wednesday it was transacted on the road between Appleby and Brampton'.[43] Fairgoers were evidently undeterred by their exclusion from the Hill. In 1919 the *Herald* reported the 'largest gathering for many years', boosted by the sale of demobilised army horses. Subsequent press reports of sales taking place on the Hill can be taken to refer not to the enclosure itself, but to the roadside verges that skirted it. Appleby Fair had become 'the annual Horse Fair on the road adjoining Gallows Hill, Appleby';[44] and for the next four decades its activities would flow around but not on its former home.[45] Appleby Borough Council, while nominally hosting a fair that no longer existed, did not recognise the one that actually took place. Not until October 1945 did any of its documents mention it.[46] Press and public might speak of 'Fair Hill'; but when in 1930 the Town Clerk inadvertently wrote the words in the Committee Minutes volume in the context of the removal of stumps of burnt whins from the enclosure, he noticed his mistake, crossed out 'Fair' and substituted 'Gallows'.[47]

---

38   *Herald*, 16 Sep. 1911.
39   *Herald*, 15 Jun. 1912.
40   The 1913 enclosure agreement between the Guarantors and Appleby Corporation is in the possession of Appleby Town Council's solicitors.
41   *Herald*, 14 Jun. 1913.
42   *Herald*, 12 Jun. 1915.
43   *Herald*, 17 Jun. 1916.
44   *Observer*, 20 Jun. 1922.
45   G. Coles, 'Appleby "New Fair"', Appleby-in-Westmorland Society newsletter, May 2003.
46   Appleby BC Committee Minutes, 1945-49, p. 1, Health & Highways, 1 Oct. 1946. A sub-committee had been appointed to investigate 'the position arising out of Appleby Fair'.
47   Appleby BC Committee Minutes, 1929-37, p. 69, Finance, 4 Mar. 1930.

Chapter 7:

Evolution: the Gypsy/Traveller Fair

What had all this to do with Gypsy/Travellers? It has recently been asserted that 'the trail of evidence shows that by Victorian times Appleby was identified as a Gypsy horse fair'.[1] There is no evidence of any such trail; but it is likely that there was always an element among those attending the Fair with horses to sell who would now be described as 'Gypsy/Traveller'. Whereas cattle and sheep normally spend their lives in large groups in one locality, usually in enclosed spaces, before making their final journey, horses are more amenable to covering long distances between grazing patches. It was hardly possible for landless itinerants to raise sheep or cattle, but they had a strong association with owning, moving and dealing in horses, and might be expected to come to a fair at which horses were traded.

Other travellers – perhaps those wintering at Natland or Wigton – came to sell pots.[2] The *Gazette* in 1836 related the tale of an 'itinerant potter', described as 'from the neighbourhood of Appleby' but more probably on his way there, who bought his goods from a factory at Whitehaven but had not even reached Bransty toll bar when his horse collapsed and died. 'He was bewailing his fate when the Earl of Lonsdale chanced to pass, heard the tale, and directed his steward to make good the loss and give the potter a horse from his Lordship's farms'.[3] The next reference is an 1873 account, which described 'the potters who mustered in great force from their encampments on the Moor' on the evening of the fair, doing a 'thriving trade';[4] and in 1890 there was 'a large encampment of the "potter tribe" on Gallows Hill and its approaches … numerous picturesque encampments among the tenants of which some of the purebred Rommany [*sic*]are to be seen'. [5] And occasional defendants among those brought before magistrates in the wake of fairs for such offences as drunk and disorderly behaviour, 'furious driving' and – in the case of Thomas Lee and Frederick Alexander in 1895 – pickpocketing, were described as 'without any fixed abode'.

But these are rarities. It may be that the 'the apparent silence about Gypsy/Travellers in late nineteenth century reports about Appleby New Fair', coupled with repeated allusions to the 'sharping fraternity' of crooked

---

1   Sagar-Musgrave and Lloyd, *Appleby Fair*, Introduction.
2   T.W. Carrick, *History of Wigton* (Carlisle, 1949) pp. 91, 123.
3   *Gazette,* 18 Jun. 1836.
4   *Herald,* 14 Jun. 1873.
5   *Penrith Advertiser,* 10 Jun. 1890.

horse dealers, 'speaks volumes' about a process of 'othering' itinerants.[6]   It may be that earlier in the century when the Kendal papers described gullible locals being hoodwinked by 'the light-fingered tribe',[7] 'the swell mob and Leeds sharpers',[8] and 'the "horse-trick" gentry', this was coded language for Gypsies.[9]   But it is hard to imagine that the horse trick could have been successfully carried out by men who were recognisably nomads, and it may be questioned whether words like 'gentry', or even 'tribe' represent anything more than the tendency of rural societies to attribute wrongdoing to gangs of outsiders. The simplest explanation for scant mention of Gypsy/Travellers in press reports of the Fair is that their part in it was peripheral as long as it was primarily for drovers.

By the mid-Victorian era, British Gypsies, after two centuries of oblivion, had begun to attract literary attention, some of it romantic, some disapproving of a way of life perceived as arcane and barbaric. Whether or not the number of families who 'took to travelling as a way of life, at least for a sizeable part of the year' was increasing,[10] it became increasingly fashionable to write about them. George Borrow's lyrical descriptions of encounters with Gypsies proved immensely and durably popular, although his travels did not take him anywhere near Appleby.[11] No more did his admirer and imitator Charles Leland, for whom Gypsies were 'the human type of this vanishing, direct love of nature, of this mute sense of rural romance',[12] nor the bilious George Smith, who saw in Gypsydom only drunkenness, brutality, dirt and dishonesty,[13] make any mention of the fairs of Westmorland. Emma Leslie's cautionary tale about the foolish servant girl who runs away with the Gypsies only to become a virtual slave at a succession of fairs is very vague about geography; but the fair 'on the borders of Scotland', almost certainly refers to Kirk Yetholm, not Appleby.[14] In his 'Autobiography of a Gypsy', Silvester Gordon Boswell, born in Blackpool in 1895, described the family travels of his young days in Wales, the Thames Estuary and the East Midlands, but

6   S. Holloway, 'Outsiders in rural society? Constructions of rurality and nature-society relations in the racialisation of English Gypsy-Travellers, 1869-1934', *Environment and Planning: Society and Space* (2003), 21, pp. 695-715.

7   *Gazette*, 17 Jun. 1843.

8   *Gazette*, 17 Jun. 1848.

9   *Gazette*, 14 Jun. 1852.

10   Mayall, *Gypsy-Travellers in 19th century Society*, p. 14.

11   G. Borrow, *Lavengro* (London, 1851), *The Romany Rye* (London, 1857), *Wild Wales* (London, 1862).

12   C.G. Leland, *The Gypsies* (London, 1882).

13   G. Smith, *Gipsy Life, being an account of our Gipsies and their Children* (London, 1880).

14   E. Leslie, *A Gypsy Against Her Will, or worth her weight in gold* (London, 1889). The genre is discussed in Jodie Matthews, 'Back where they belong: Gypsies, kidnapping and assimilation in Victorian children's literature', *Romani Studies 5*, 20.2 (2010), pp. 137-159.

not the North West.[15] George Hall, the 'Gypsy's Parson', whose book asked 'Where is a Gypsy if not at a horse fair?', listed the principal fairs, but he too made no reference to Appleby, despite a lyrical description of 'rings of dark figures squatting around the blazing logs' at nearby Brough Hill fair: 'a feast for the eyes of a lover of nomads was this array of firelit faces set against a background of caravans, stone walls and mountains'.[16] T.W. Thompson, the Kendal Grammar School and Cambridge-educated gypsiologist, the first of whose many papers appeared in 1911,[17] and his associate F.S. Atkinson, who when still at school wrote lovingly about the Natland settlement, were also silent on Appleby Fair, although it was in their native county.[18] We may reasonably infer that the event was not yet particularly associated with Gypsies.

It is clear, however, that as horse-trading became paramount, Gypsy/Travellers were a growing element at Appleby New Fair. The point at which it effectively became a Gypsy Horse Fair can be with some certainty located to the Edwardian decade, 1901-10. Scattered entries in baptismal registers indicate a developing trend. The first baptism at St Michael's, Bongate, of a child whose address was registered as 'New Fair Hill' was on 10 June 1888;[19] Joseph Miller was son of Isabella and Joseph, described as a 'Hawker'. In 1891 the same couple had another son, Jacob, baptised at St Margaret & St James', Long Marton; his birthplace was given as Brampton, and his father's occupation as 'General Dealer'.[20] In June 1902 the vicar of St Lawrence's, Appleby christened Naomi Gray daughter of John, a 'Showman', and his wife Sarah, of 'Fair Hill, Appleby', and the following year christened Thomas Lee, whose birthplace was simply recorded as 'Appleby', son of Edward, a 'Husker', and Redingel.[21] In July 1912 the rector of Long Marton recorded his private baptism of Jane, daughter of Susannah Cannon of Brampton; the father was Thomas Smith, 'Horse Dealer' of 'Fair Hill, Appleby'.

Press reports confirm the trend. In 1901 'women were also plentiful, mostly of the Romany type, and various encampments could be seen dotting the moor and lining the fairground'.[22] In 1907, when there was heavy rain,

15   S. G. Boswell, *The Book of Boswell; the Autobiography of a Gypsy*, ed. J. Seymour (1970), pp. 33-55. Although commonly referred to in the press by his first name (frequently spelled 'Sylvester') he preferred Gordon. He was part of an established dynasty: see V. S. Morwood, *Our Gipsies in City, Tent and Van* (1885).

16   Rev G. Hall, *The Gypsy's Parson* (London, 1915), pp. 269-278.

17   T.W. Thompson, 'Storms and Interludes', *JGLS*, IV.4 (1911), 'Affairs of Egypt, 1909' *JGLS*, V.2 (1911).

18   F.S. Atkinson, 'Gypsies in Westmorland' *The Kendalian* (1909), pp. 12-17. Thompson and Atkinson co-wrote the article in *JGLS*, V.2.

19   Kendal Archive Centre, Appleby St. Michael, Register of Baptisms, 1857-1975. After 1885 Fair Hill was within Bongate.

20   Kendal Archive Centre, Long Marton Registers on film JAC 1723. There is an earlier Miller baptism from 1875; the father, Isaac is designated a 'potter'.

21   Kendal Archive Centre, Appleby St. Lawrence Registers on film JAC 1717.

22   *Herald*, 15 Jun. 1901.

'the potters who had taken up a comfortable position with their wandering horses, in a wide ditch well up the Brampton road, had probably the best time of it … and complacently cooked and ate their savouries, and tended their offspring, heedless of the prying eyes of an army of onlookers'.[23] In 1912 a scene of 'caravans and living huts' stretched along the roadsides was described as:

> … similar to that of Brough Hill, only on a smaller scale. There were more of the potter tribe than ever before. Dotted here and there was the good woman of the "home" standing over a wood fire, the fuel for which had evidently been taken from nearby fences and trees. Further down the road horses were tied to the fences.[24]

'W', writing in the *Penrith Observer* in the wake of the 1914 Fair, considered it 'changed for the better … The gypsy tribes seem as numerous as ever and there is evidently a great reunion at this fair … It was a most peaceful scene, a well-behaved gathering, and a great contrast to days gone by, when fights in plenty ended the day's business'.[25]

But not all who witnessed these scenes viewed them in so favourable a light. There can be little doubt that a desire to divest themselves of any responsibility for them was a factor in the agreement of the commoners headed by Lords Hothfield (Figure 12) – whose ancestor had brought the Fair into being – and Lord Lonsdale to bestow Gallows Hill on Appleby Borough Corporation. Although neither the donors nor the recipients made any reference in writing to the Fair's existence, in September 1911 the Mayor, John Sewell Rigg (Figure 13), made a point of praising Hothfield to his fellow councillors for 'assisting in driving away the nomads on Gallows Hill, who had been a source of vexation and annoyance'.[26] On his feet again at the mayoral banquet two months later, he reiterated his satisfaction: Appleby Council could now 'bar from the Hill the nomads, who had always been a source of annoyance'.[27] That Rigg himself was a dealer in horses may or may not have influenced his view. The question of whether 'the nomads' might be regarded as part of 'the public' for whose enjoyment the land was being conveyed to the Council seems not to have arisen.

But if there were any hopes that, once locked out of the Hill, Appleby Fairgoers would follow the example of others in slipping quietly into history, and their annual arrival become but a folk memory, they were not fulfilled. In June 1915, with Britain now at war, the *Observer* reported that the Fair

---

23   *Observer,* 18 Jun. 1907.
24   *Herald,* 15 Jun. 1912. For the connotations of 'potter', see chapter 1, p. 4.
25   *Observer,* 16 Jun. 1914.
26   *Herald,* 16 Sep. 1911. The occasion was the Council meeting mentioned in chapter 6.
27   *Observer,* 14 Nov. 1911. A former hotelier and prominent local Conservative, Rigg had been Captain of the Appleby Fire Brigade, whose horses he supplied. M. Clowes, *Appleby Fire Brigade: Johnny Rigg and the first Fireman of Appleby* (Kirkby Stephen, 2014).

Figure 12. Henry Tufton, first Baron Hothfield (1844-1926). Photographed from the original by John Tillotson. Reproduced by kind permission of the sixth Baron Hothfield.

Figure 13. John Sewell Rigg, mayor of Appleby 1910-12. Photographed by Keith Morgan from the original. Reproduced by kind permission of Appleby Town Council.

'did not seem to have lost any of its popularity ... as a spectacular affair ... The early trains brought large numbers of people to the fair, and those not purely on business bent found a great measure of amusement in watching the nomadic tribes which always frequent these fairs proceeding with their domestic arrangements and decking out the youngsters in the festive garments characteristic of these red letter days in their lives'.[28] The voluntary military service of some Gypsy/Travellers in the Great War is now well documented; but most were beyond the reach of conscription.[29] It seems certain that during the war, with a much reduced attendance of 'farmers and the general public',[30] they consolidated their dominance of the Fair, which was increasingly being perceived as 'a rendezvous' for 'the caravan fraternity, whose encampment stretched along the road for over a mile'.[31]

Reports in 1919 and 1920 paint a similar picture of extensive roadside camping and busy trading around the Hill, even if 'the good old fair times,

28   *Observer,* 15 Jun. 1915.
29   *Boswell,* 71-80. J. Keet-Black, 'Gypsies didn't go to war – did they?' *Romany Routes,* vol. 7, no. 1 (Dec. 2004).
30   *Herald,* 16 Jun. 1917
31   *Herald,* 17 Jun. 1916.

with their excitement and what might be called romance, will never return'.[32]
In 1921, the *Herald* reported: 'not for many years has there been such an
attendance of the fraternity who enjoy the simple but often-times well-
provided life in touring the country in caravans and on flat carts'.[33] The
Observer meanwhile remarked that 'on the afternoon of the fair the younger
girls enjoy parading the fair ground in all their rakish finery, the principal items
of which appear to be high-legged tan boots, striped coloured dresses and
dazzling hair ribbons'.[34] The innovation in 1922 of Whit Monday 'trotting'
– harness races patronised by local enthusiasts and Gypsy/Travellers alike,
and soon reportedly attracting crowds of several thousand – was another
factor drawing people into the town around the time of the New Fair; 'by rail
and road people flocked into Appleby from all points of the compass'.[35]

New Fair newspaper reports from the inter-war years, albeit mannered
and repetitious, depicted a romantic scene, evoking 'the pages of George
Borrow's immortal works': the scent of woodsmoke and frying bacon, the
'constant clatter of horses hoofs as they were being galloped and shown off by
their dark-eyed dealers', and 'sturdy lads waltzing with the brightly arrayed
lasses in the lights of many camp fires'.[36] It was now 'more a gathering of the
clans than anything else'.[37] The same was said of Brough Hill in Autumn, 'not
so much a fair at which animals are bought and sold as it is a conglomeration
of customs and traditions dating back hundreds of years' of 'those charming
rogues the gipsies'.[38] Discordant notes were occasionally struck, as in a
bilious 1931 comment on Gypsy fortune-tellers. The 'veriest looking slut',
could with 'various sartorial accoutrements ... transform herself into an
oriental princess ... thus arrayed she poises herself at a point of vantage from
which her smile intercepts those giddy damsels who have a desire to peep
into the future and hear of a dark man crossing a fair woman, a journey, a
huge fortune and an 'andsome 'usband'.[39]

A list of places whence in 1929 caravans had come to Appleby – Darlington,
Skipton, Bradford, Poulton-le-Fylde, Lancaster and Carnforth – confirms
the evidence of court reports: miscreants brought before the magistrates
by the police charged with offences committed during the fair were usually
from northern England.[40] Bernard Renwick, labourer, convicted in 1933

32   *Herald*, 12 Jun. 1920.
33   *Herald*, 11 Jun. 1921.
34   *Observer*, 14 Jun. 1921.
35   *Herald*, 5 Jun. 1925. The event, which then included sports, was reported as having been 'started
       by the ex-service men of Appleby only three years ago'. Managed by a local committee, the trotting
       continues to be held on the Holme Farm meadow, a natural amphitheatre on the river bank close
       to the town centre.
36   *Herald*, 11 Jun. 1927.
37   *Observer*, 20 Jun. 1922.
38   *Observer*, 20 Sep. 1924.
39   *Observer*, 20 Jun. 1931.
40   *Herald*, 15 Jun. 1929.

for being drunk and disorderly in charge of a horse and cart, came from Bishop Auckland, while Thomas Smith, hawker, who fought with police after being ejected from the Grapes Inn and resisted the attempts of his friends to get him away on a flat cart, was from Bolton, Lancashire.[41] Two significant changes attracted regular press comment. One was the growing prevalence of 'palatial motor drawn caravans' which, albeit 'spotlessly clean' and 'equipped with many modern labour saving devices' were 'sadly lacking in romance'.[42] The second change, remarked on as early as 1922, was the scarcity of 'real gypsies'.[43] 'Romany folk … distinguishable by their dusky skins, pearly teeth and flashing eyes',[44] 'with real gipsy blood in their veins',[45] were said to be a rarity. Forty years later much the same was being identified as a development of 'recent years': it was only thanks to just 'a few Romany gypsies among the hundreds of nomadic folk, notable for their brilliant dark eyes, swarthy skins and glittering ear-rings' that the Fair still 'retained a romantic atmosphere'.[46] The golden age of Appleby's 'traditional' Romani Horse Fair proves to be a will o' the wisp: it might, if anywhere, be located in the first two decades of the 20th century, but it was disappearing almost as soon as it began.

41   *Herald*, 17 Jun. 1933.
42   *Herald*, 14 Jun. 1930.
43   *Herald*, 17 Jun. 1922.
44   *Herald*, 13 Jun. 1931.
45   *Herald*, 17 Jun. 1933.
46   *Herald*, 14 Jun. 1964.

Chapter 8:

World War II and After: 'The New Fair Has Outlived Its Usefulness'

In September 1939 – in stark contrast with August 1914 – the outbreak of war had long been expected: within days, in anticipation of German bombers which would not be seen for another year, evacuees from Tyneside arrived in Westmorland. Several agricultural shows in villages that were in any event unlikely targets were summarily cancelled.[1] A week before the usual date for Brough Hill Fair a terse notice in the *Herald* announced that 'owing to the outbreak of War' it would not be held until further notice.[2] In the wake of this non-event, members of the Cumberland and North Westmorland branch of the NFU expressed their disappointment. Hundreds of people had turned up unaware of the cancellation; but by whose authority had the order had been made?[3] This may have been a rhetorical question, since the answer was obvious. The notice had appeared above the name of C.E. Fordyce of the estate office, Appleby Castle, acting on behalf of the second Baron Hothfield, the owner of Brough Hill, to whose Clifford ancestor the fair charter had been granted by Edward III.

Would Appleby New fair suffer a similar fate? Westmorland County Council officers evidently thought so. The log book of St Lawrence's School recorded the receipt of a telegram on 7 June 1940 from the education office 'cancelling annual holiday for Appleby Horse Fair next week'.[4] Leonard Chapman, headmaster of the council school noted: 'For the first time in living memory of local residents the school was not closed. The holiday, granted as usual by the managers, was cancelled because of the war'.[5] But if any such order was received by Long Marton School, it was either quickly rescinded or simply ignored: on 12 June, the head teacher noted as usual: 'School will be closed tomorrow owing to Appleby New Fair'.[6] Whatever officials in Kendal imagined, Gypsy/Travellers and their horses had arrived unhindered in the Eden Valley. 'Silverpen' of the *Herald* noted that, in contrast to Brough Hill Fair, 'rather arbitrarily closed as a wartime measure', the New Fair had

---

1   *Herald,* 16 Sep. 1939.

2   *Herald,* 23 Sep. 1939.

3   *Herald,* 7 Oct. 1939. *Gazette,* same date.

4   Log Book of St. Lawrence's School, Appleby, 1913-47, 7 Jun. 1940.

5   Kendal Archive Centre, WDS/71/4/2, Log Book of Appleby Central Council School, 1937-48, 11-12 Jun. 1940.

6   Kendal Archive Centre, WDS/127/2/2, Log Book of Long Marton School, 1902-41, 12 Jun. 1940.

taken place as normal, with the usual 'white tents' and 'quite an array of county police'. He speculated that this might be because its midsummer timing meant that there was no need of artificial light and camp fires for the kindly Romany folk who 'looked like chocolate soldiers, so swarthy was their colouring and so sweltering was the heat'.[7] The *Gazette* more prosaically reported a fair of 'reasonable proportions' doing a 'fair amount of genuine business', while noting the 'absence of large bodies of the sight-seeing element'.[8]

If it had been seriously imagined that camp fires would provide guidance to enemy bombers in the autumnal night skies, by September 1940 such fears had been put in perspective. 'Authority relented' and 'the road to Brough Hill was lined on each side with private cars and motor buses of all hues'.[9] 'The gipsy people were not so numerous as they often are', but there was a 'larger gathering than usual of the farming fraternity' in the 'good-humoured crowd', reflecting the demand for agricultural horses with two-year-old Clydesdales fetching up to £60. There were no further suggestions that the Eden Valley's horse fairs might be prevented from taking place. Local schools closed as usual for Appleby Fair in 1941. The shortage of newsprint limited press coverage, with the main focus on Appleby Methodists' 'old established' open-air meeting on the Sunday of the Fair, featuring preaching, prayer and singing to the accompaniment of a portable organ; 'the usual interest was maintained, large numbers lining the roadsides'.[10] Anecdotal recollections confirm that, spiritually refreshed, some of the Gypsy/Travellers would repair to the town to drink, and older local children would wait outside the pubs for ten o'clock closing in the hope of seeing a brawl.[11]

But perceptions of Appleby Fair were changed by the Second World War. In 1939 local farmers resented being deprived of the opportunity for buying horses; by the end of the War some at least had decided that 'the New Fair had outlived its usefulness'.[12] The future lay in tractors, not horses; and the ethos of a disciplined 'War Ag.' countryside perhaps fostered growing intolerance of nomadic lifestyles beyond the reach of official control. Shortly after the 1945 New Fair, which had evoked grumbles that 'the camping fraternity' arrived a week early,[13] a National Farmers' Union meeting complained that numbers of campers had been 'far above anything ever known': it seemed that 'the whole horse-dealing fraternity of the North of England had decided to make Appleby New Fair their V.E. reunion'.[14] Concluding that 'it was time

---

7   *Herald*, 15 Jun. 1940.
8   *Gazette*, 15 Jun. 1940.
9   *Herald*, 5 Oct. 1940.
10   *Herald*, 14 Jun. 1941, 13 Jun. 1942.
11   See Appendix 2.
12   *Herald*, 16 Mar. 1946.
13   *Herald*, 5 Jun. 1946: letter from 'A Ratepayer'.
14   *Herald*, 14 Jul. 1945.

the fair was done away with', the branch wrote to Appleby Corporation to that effect.

In the Moot Hall Council Chamber the case for abolition was argued by Aldermen Slack and Dawson, the one an Appleby farmer, the other an agricultural supplier living on the road to Brampton (Figure 7). Animus towards an occasion with which they had lifelong familiarity may have been coloured by a perceived contrast in the fairgoers' contribution to victory and that of their own families: in August and September 1944 sons of Slack and Dawson had been respectively killed over Germany and wounded and taken prisoner at Arnhem. They persuaded their fellow councillors that the Fair had now 'no business' in Appleby.[15] While the 'lost charter' was being sought, the Borough invoked the assistance of Westmorland County Council, which early in 1946 batted the issue back. Their Clerk reported he had made 'a thorough investigation' into the right to hold the Fair; he concluded that the 1871 Fairs Act empowered the Home Secretary to order abolition, but that representation must first be made by the local authorities, in this instance not Westmorland County Council, but Appleby Borough and North Westmorland Rural District Councils.[16] After a debate in which the Fair was described as 'little more than a holiday camp of an undesirable nature', a threat to public health and an 'unprecedented nuisance',[17] Appleby Council resolved to write to the Home Office. The reply advised that abolition would require the consent of the 'owners' of the Fair and a declaration by local magistrates that its termination 'would be to the convenience and advantage of the public'.[18]

Even as Appleby Borough Council pondered the practicalities of claiming ownership, eloquent local support for the Fair was emerging. A series of letters to the *Herald* protested that Appleby councillors were taking it upon themselves to destroy an ancient tradition without gauging public opinion in either the town or the neighbouring parishes in which most of the camping took place.[19] Long Marton Parish Council told Appleby Council that 'all the nuisances complained of would be overcome' if 'the borough would throw open the Fair Hill to campers', and urged North Westmorland RDC to 'prevent the abolition of Brampton Fair' and 'provide the necessary water and sanitation'.[20] The *Herald* gave extensive coverage to the 1946 Fair, quoting a Gypsy/Traveller, 72-year old Miss Jessie Adams of Stockton, whose family had attended Appleby Fair 'for generations'. She said that they now had a permanent home, but looked forward all year to taking to the road to meet

15 Herald, 15 Sep. 1945. See Appendix 3 for suggestive evidence that controversy over the Fair's future raised its media profile.
16 Kendal Archive Centre, Westmorland County Council Minutes (1945-6) pp. 758-9, 15 Feb. 1946.
17 *Herald*, 16 Mar. 1946.
18 *Herald*, 18 May and 22 Jun. 1946.
19 *Herald*, 6 Apr. 1946, letter signed by 'Common Sense', 'Fairplay' and 'Progress'.
20 *Herald*, 8 Jun. 1946.

old friends. In the same issue, the paper's columnist expressed the view that:

> The old fairs will die from natural causes if left alone, and, as an old time curiosity I favour this course, more especially if it will mean less harassing of the gipsies, a strange but romantic and kindly people, made more familiar to us by the writings of Lady Eleanor Smith and others.[21]

Ray Burton, secretary of Appleby Labour Party, thought that 'Fair Week should be a period of festivity, rejoicing and friendship' with a mayoral reception for campers,[22] and accused the town council of representing the interests of an 'elete' (sic) which preferred 'to see workers and nomads a good distance away from them at all times except when service is required for low wages'.[23] The local branch of the National Union of Railwaymen, of which his father Isaac was secretary, announced its support for the Fair on the grounds that it brought extra work to the railway.[24] A former Appleby resident who now lived in West Yorkshire expressed his 'disgust' with the attitude of councillors who 'seem to regard the Council as a private business concern'.[25]

Nevertheless, when the Mayor of Appleby, accompanied by Aldermen Dawson and Slack, the Town Clerk and the Borough Surveyor, met with two Westmorland County Councillors and two North Westmorland Rural District Councillors in October 1946, the meeting resolved to ask the RDC 'to co-operate with Appleby Borough Council in taking steps to abolish the Appleby Fair, or alternatively to co-operate with the Borough Council in making suitable rules for the regulation of the Fair'. But at its November 1946 meeting North Westmorland RDC accepted neither request; instead it voted not to support abolition, and recommended that Fair Hill be thrown open to campers during fair week.[26] By the end of March 1947 Appleby BC had backed down so far as to discuss with its Gallows Hill tenants how much reduction in rental they would demand if this were to happen, and to set up a Fair Hill Sub-Committee on which Alderman Dawson declined to serve.[27] It resolved to talk to 'influential members who attend the June Fair and Representatives of the Showman's Guild',[28] and reported 'certain suggestions' in the light of which it was instructed to 'prepare a scheme'.[29]

---

21   *Herald*, 15 Jun. 1946. Several of the melodramatic novels of Lady Eleanor Smith (1902-45) had gypsy themes, e.g. *Romany* (1935). Some were filmed: crucial to the plot of *The Man In Grey*, a hugely popular British bodice-ripper of 1943, is a gypsy fortune-teller.

22   *Herald*, 22 Jun. 1946, letter from R. Burton.

23   *Herald*, 6 Jul. 1946, letter from R. Burton.

24   *Herald*, 20 Jul. 1946, letter from S. Holmes.

25   *Herald*, 13 Jul. 1946.

26   *Herald*, 16 Nov. 1946

27   Appleby BC Committee Minutes, 1945-49, p. 155, meeting of Health & Highways Committee, 31 Mar. 1947.

28   Ibid., pp. 174-5, meeting of Fair Hill Sub-Committee, 30 May 1947.

29   Ibid., pp. 180-1, Fair Hill Sub-Committee, 10 Jun. 1947, Health & Highways Committee, 30 Jun. 1947; *Herald*, 12 Jul. 1947.

The scheme, unveiled in September 1947, envisaged the opening of Gallows Hill for a week, with a tariff of charges for vehicles, a cinder track to be built there on which horses could be 'shown', rather than on the highway, and the provision of water tanks and 'sanitary conveniences'. There were to be discussions with Westmorland CC, North Westmorland RDC and the Ministry of Works, 'seeking co-operation in the proposed scheme both financially and otherwise'.[30]

Apart from improved provision of water, little progress was made, but as late as 1 June 1948, the Fair Hill Committee was planning for the following week water tanks, and temporary and appropriate signage to direct campers off the roads and on to the Hill.[31] At the last moment they decided to put off the attempt for a year; the state of the ground following 'recent heavy rain' was the stated reason,[32] but the postponement may have had more to do with a meeting with Gypsy/Traveller representatives, 'Messrs Birmingham, Hudson and Stewart'. That when 'the Committee explained to them the Council's scheme for providing accommodation on Fair-Hill' the reception was less than enthusiastic may be inferred from the belated decision that there would be a mayoral visit for the purpose of 'explaining the proposals to the people attending the fair'.[33] On the Tuesday evening of Fair Week the Mayor, Harold Knight, toured the roads around the Hill in a loud speaker van; he 'stood in a magnificent high-powered roadster belonging to one of the leaders of the fair people' and addressed an open-air meeting of campers. He assured them that up to £5,000 would be spent on transforming Fair Hill into 'a proper camping site', with roads, piped water and 'sanitary conveniences'. He urged campers to 'support the Council and use the site: there would be a charge for sites, but campers 'would be able to come when they wished and stay as long as they liked'. 'Mr Birmingham, one of the fair attenders who has been consulting with the Council', spoke in support, and 'there were cries of, "Yes, we'll go," ... Thus after several years of uncertainty, it seems the Fair is to take a new lease of life'.[34]

A year later nothing had changed. The post-war years of the creation of the welfare state and the National Health Service were years, too, of rationing, intermittent financial crisis and austerity. To transform Fair Hill Appleby Borough Council sought an £1800 loan from the Ministry of Health, and was referred to the Ministry of Town & Country Planning.[35] Council minutes in March 1949 recorded that 'the Town Clerk reported an interview with

---

30   Ibid., pp. 206-7, Health & Highways Committee, 29 Sep. 1947; pp. 243-4, 259-60, Fair Hill Sub-Committee, 2 Jan. 1948, 30 Jan. 1948.
31   Ibid., p. 317-8, meeting of Fair Hill Sub- Committee, 1 Jun. 1948.
32   *Herald*, 12 Jun. 1948.
33   Appleby BC Committee Minutes, 1945-49, p. 321, meeting of Fair Hill Sub- Committee, 4 Jun. 1948.
34   *Herald*, 12 Jun. 1948.
35   Appleby BC Committee Minutes, 1945-49, p. 155, meeting of Fair Hill Sub-Committee, 1 Mar. 1949.

the Regional Controller of the Ministry' but added nothing further. Fair Hill remained locked and unimproved. As the *Herald* reported in 1952, there had been 'no further progress' in the project 'for when the Council applied for a loan from the Government it was refused'.[36] So the Fair of the 1950s followed familiar lines and was reported in familiar phrases, usually accompanied by picturesque photographs

Figure 14. Gypsy/Traveller campers near Fair Hill, c. 1956. Photograph by Gordon Wood. Reproduced by kind permission of Appleby-in-Westmorland Society.

of 'crowds and caravans'. In 1951 the *Herald* correspondent was thrilled to discover that one of the 'more luxurious' caravans was occupied by the Irish tenor Josef Locke, who was combining a visit to the Fair with a golfing holiday. The celebrity duly obliged with a quote: 'It's powerful, it's great'.[37] In 1952 'one of the potters' reminisced about the 'old days' when 'Appleby was known as the "courting fair" among his people, to be followed by the "marriage fair" at Brough Hill' but lamented that things had changed. 'Now the young folk think more of motor car dealing than horses, and prance around in flashy suits with padded shoulders, coloured socks and soft shoes. Why, they have forgotten the old gypsy dances, and only care for jitterbugging and the like'.[38]

Some traditions lived on, however. In 1955, a 22-year old 'general dealer' from Blackpool was fined £2 after pleading guilty to being 'fighting mad' in the King's Head Hotel, Appleby. Another young 'general dealer' from Shildon was less co-operative. Stopped by police for drunken driving, he refused to be examined by a local doctor, whom he claimed to have seen drinking in the same public house as himself. He was fined £20 with £3 13s 6d costs, and banned from driving for three years.[39] In 1957 the *Herald* columnist 'Mercury' commented that the Fair was now flourishing 'as never before in all its long history. The size of the assembly this year – not only the campers themselves in their hundreds of caravans, but even more so the throng of sightseers – had to be seen to be believed'. It was 'hard to believe that ten years ago a proposal to abolish the ancient horse fair was in the air' (Figure 14).[40]

---

36   *Herald*, 14 Jun. 1952.
37   *Herald*, 16 Jun. 1951. 'Josef Locke' was the stage name of Joseph McLaughlin (1917-99).
38   *Herald*, 14 Jun. 1952. This alleged interview was repeated, with slight variations, in 1953.
39   *Herald*, 11 Jun. 1955.
40   *Herald*, 15 Jun. 1957.

Chapter 9:

'Appleby New Fair Should Be Abolished'

But a year later the same *Herald* column remarked that the fair was 'a very mixed blessing' for Appleby, whose residents 'must often consider that the best thing that could happen to the New Fair would be for it to cease altogether'.[1] This change of tune was perhaps symptomatic of dwindling local tolerance of the annual Gypsy/Traveller influx. It had become a local article of faith that each Appleby Fair was bigger than the last. Press reports routinely made the assertion, sometimes supported by speculative and unattributed figures. So in 1948, the New Fair attracted 'between 6,000 and 7,000 nomadic people';[2] in 1959 there was an 'Appleby gathering larger than ever', with over 3,000 'horse dealers, gypsies and potter folk.'[3] In 1961, with 'over 2,000 campers', the fair was 'bigger than ever'.[4] The received local wisdom was that the popularity of Appleby's Whit Monday harness racing was bringing in more Gypsy/Travellers who would remain in the area until the Fair.[5] The published names of horse-owners at the races, as well as odd press references to 'tinkers', confirm a growing Irish element among them.[6]

Whether or not numbers at Appleby Fair really were increasing, post-war housing development meant that the daily surge of humanity to and from the roadside camping area to the river and the town passed close to many more homes than previously. And with running water and inside lavatories now the norm for the settled population even in rural Westmorland, sanitary arrangements heavily dependent on trees, bushes and hedgerows attracted adverse comment not previously reported. Traffic too was a growing source of grievance in the 1950s. Fairgoers' motor-drawn caravans were occupying more space than before, and the general surge in vehicle ownership meant that the Fair increasingly obstructed both local and long-haul road traffic, by virtue both of temporary road-side settlement and of horse shows and sales on the Sands, which formed a short stretch of the A66 trunk road. Nor perhaps did even part-time nomadism sit well with public acceptance of a planned

---

1   *Herald*, 14 Jun. 1958
2   *Herald*, 12 Jun. 1948.
3   *Herald*, 13 Jun. 1959.
4   *Herald*, 17 Jun. 1961
5   *Herald*, 4 Jun. 1955, '9,000 people at Appleby races'.
6   *Herald*, 14 Jun. 1952. Cf. *Observer* 15 Jun. 1920, when the presence of an Irishman, 'the real genuine article' at the fair, had occasioned comment.

social environment within a framework of increasing owner occupancy.[7] Yet the romantic appeal of the Fair to onlookers was evidently growing and spreading: in 1961 'as usual the fair attracted thousands of visitors who came by car and coach to throng the country roads and the number of American and foreign accents showed that the fair is fast becoming a tourist attraction'.[8]

But by then local authority discussions on its future had again been set in train. In the wake of the 1960 Fair, a letter was received by North Westmorland RDC from fifteen local landowners, among them Richard Jackson Dawson, protesting about 'the filth in our fields and lanes'. It was followed by a similar petition from Long Marton and Brampton residents.[9] The Medical Officer of Health, while expressing willingness to 'lend my support on public health grounds', thought the problem was in the first instance one for lawyers. 'Surely it could be proven whether there is a valid right, by Charter or otherwise to hold Appleby New Fair, where it may be held, and for how long? And are there not legal remedies against the breach of these terms?'[10] But this was familiar barren ground, which the County, District and Borough Councils did not choose to till again. Instead, after discussions with the police, in January 1961 they decided to revive the aspirations of the late 1940s to get the fair off the roads; a 'Scheme' was to be prepared for 'providing facilities on the Gallows Hill site'.[11]

A year passed. Armed with a blueprint for equipping Fair Hill with an access road, a three-inch water main and temporary sanitation at an estimated cost of £5,000, the various councils optimistically decided in January 1962 to approach the Showman's Guild in Glasgow for a contribution.[12] 'I am sure you will agree', wrote R.C. Howell, Clerk of North Westmorland RDC, 'that the present practice of camping on the roadside verges is undesirable and unhygienic'.[13] The reply informed him that 'the hawkers etc. with whom you are mainly concerned in this matter are not in any way concerned with our Association'.[14] Nothing changed in 1962; nor in 1963, when 'Gypsies and potter folk congregated in large numbers ... their caravans forming long lines on either side of the Appleby-Long Marton road'.[15] 'No course of action was decided upon', wrote Howell to K.S. Himsworth, Clerk of Westmorland CC,

---

7   Post-1951 Conservative governments might claim to be setting the people free from red tape, but this did not extend to Gypsy-Travellers, whose ability to roam at will was further curtailed by the 1960 Caravan Sites and Control of Development Act.

8   *Herald*, 17 Jun. 1961.

9   Kendal Archive Centre, WSRDNW 3/1 Box 6, Bundle of Appleby Fair Correspondence, 1960-69. Letter to North Westmorland Rural District Council from Sarah Atkinson of Hangingshaw and fourteen others, 21 Jul. 1960.

10 Ibid., letter to NWRDC from Frank Madge , MOH for Combined Districts, 26 Jul. 1960.

11 Ibid., Minutes of meeting at Appleby Shire Hall, 18 Jan. 1961.

12 Ibid., Minutes of meeting at Appleby Shire Hall, 30 Jan. 1962.

13 Ibid., letter from R.C. Howell to A.C. Allen, Scottish Secretary of Showman's Guild, 2 Feb 1962.

14 Ibid., letter from M.E. Wills, Joint Secretary to R.C. Howell, 16 Feb 1962.

15 *Herald*, 15 Jun. 1963.

in July 1964 after yet another meeting of assorted councillors and police. 'The issues involved and the various methods suggested for dealing with the problem were rather difficult to enforce'.[16]

But rumblings of local discontent were growing louder. In the wake of the 1964 fair, Frank Shaw, the new and opinionated editor of the *Herald*, commented that this 'vast invasion', although 'no doubt admired' as a 'bustling, lusty relic of a former age', left an 'appalling mess'. He quoted the local Medical Officer of Health's expressed concern about 'a foul and dangerous polluted area'; and advertised a forthcoming meeting of Brampton and Long Marton residents 'to do something about it'.[17] The following week a front-page report of the meeting, headlined in capitals 'Appleby New Fair Should Be Abolished', related how '50 or more residents living in the vicinity of the Fair', with County, District and Borough councillors in attendance, complained about the filth and 'an invasion of people just as obnoxious as Mods and Rockers'. Following renewed speculation as to the whereabouts of 'the charter', which 'could possibly be in the hands of Lord Hothfield's solicitors', the meeting 'by an overwhelming majority' supported a motion that 'every aspect should be looked into to see if the event could be abolished'.[18] The National Union of Public Employees weighed in, complaining that 'no amount of money can reasonably compensate our members for the obnoxious task which they have performed ... may we enquire whether consideration is being given to alternative arrangements?'[19]

Westmorland County Council referred the matter to its Roads and Bridges Sub-Committee,[20] which in turn referred it to a North Eastern Divisional Committee, which convened at Appleby Shire Hall in February 1965. Chaired by W.J. Dent of Kirkby Stephen, a Westmorland county alderman, it included two Anglican clergy, the Rev. A.G.W. Dixon, vicar of Appleby and a borough councillor, and the Rev. H. Sawrey, vicar of Orton. It reported:

> The Committee were of the opinion that it would be in the public interest to seek the abolition of Appleby Fair because of (a) the present pollution of the countryside due to the lack of adequate sanitary facilities, (b) congestion of traffic near the Fair Hill and on the approaches to and from the A66.[21]

They recommended 'that the Council approve in principle the abolition of the Appleby New Fair and authorise such action to be taken to this end as

16   Appleby Fair Bundle, letter from R Howell to K. Himsworth, 31 Jul. 1964.
17   *Herald*, 20 Jun. 1964.
18   *Herald*, 27 Jun. 1964.
19   Appleby Fair Bundle, letter from D. Packham, NUPE Area Officer, Jesmond to the Westmorland County Surveyor, 5 Oct. 1964.
20   WCC Minutes (1964-5) pp. 504, 512, 666, Roads & Bridges Sub-Committee, 18 Jun., 16 Jul., 18 Dec.1964.
21   WCC Minutes (1965-6) pp. 98, 103, Roads & Bridges Sub-Committee, 19 Mar. 1965.

is appropriate and open to the Council'. On 30 April 1965 Westmorland CC duly accepted the recommendation, rejecting an amendment that there should first be consultations with the RDC as the sanitary authority and with 'representatives of people attending the Fair'.[22] A month later Appleby Borough Council's Health and Housing Committee voted by four to three to recommend the full council to 'support Westmorland County Council's efforts to abolish the Fair'.[23]

22   Ibid., Full Council, p. 169, 30 Apr. 1965.
23   Appleby BC Minutes 1965-66, p. 10, 31 May 1965. Post 1962 minutes have not yet been archived, and are stored in the Clerk's Office at the Moot Hall, Appleby-in-Westmorland.

Chapter 10:

The Saving of Appleby Fair, 1965-66

Judith Okely would subsequently remark on how, when 'Gorgio authorities tried to close the Appleby Fair' they were foiled by a display of Traveller 'solidarity' and 'overall unity'.[1] In support of this contention she cited the autobiographical reminiscences of Gordon Boswell, published in 1970. In fact, the seventy-five year old Traveller patriarch made no reference to the part he had played, though his editor added a note on Boswell's key role in persuading 'local councils' to a 'change of mind'.[2] The author of the dramatic story of how 'the swift and energetic action of a mere handful of heroic people' saved Appleby Fair and returned it to its former Fair Hill location was Richard Wade, assistant secretary of the Gypsy Lore Society, in his 1966 article in the society's journal.[3] Wade's hero was Boswell, 'aristocrat of the Romany race', to honorary membership of whose family he was subsequently admitted.[4]

Wade acknowledged too the crucial role of a scion of Westmorland's most celebrated aristocratic family, Captain Anthony Lowther, who as a Westmorland County councillor had proposed the defeated amendment calling for discussions with fairgoers, and was credited by the *Herald* with making 'a lone attempt' to save the fair.[5] At the 1947 Fair a Gypsy woman 'reminiscing in her old-world tent', recalled 'the good old days' when 'the late Lord Lonsdale used to go and dine among them … invite some of the hawkers for a day's coursing … give them £1 apiece and buy the best dog they had shown him'.[6] Now in 1965 the current Earl's brother visited the environs of Fair Hill, accompanied by his mother Muriel, Viscountess Lowther, credited by Wade with 'painstaking research' in support of the Fair,[7] and his wife and five year old daughter, for strategic campfire discussions with 'Gypsies and dealers'. Boswell was not present, but it was he who, accompanied by the 'good padre' Father Caton, Roman Catholic priest of Kirkby Stephen, at 10.30 the following morning, Wednesday 9 June, led a

---

1   Okely, *Traveller Gypsies*, pp. 198-200.
2   *The Book of Boswell*, p. 191.
3   Wade, 'Saving of Appleby Fair'. He effectively trailed the article on 22 Jun. 1965 in a long letter to the *Penrith Observer*.
4   M. Shaw, *Narrating Gypsies, Telling Travellers* (Umea, 2006), p. 87.
5   *Herald*, 12 Jun. 1965.
6   *Herald*, 14 Jun. 1947. She would be referring to the 'Yellow Earl', Hugh, fifth Lord Lonsdale, who had died in 1946, about whom many stories were told, some of them true.
7   Viscountess Lowther's research seems to have amounted to re-discovering that the 1685 Charter had nothing to do with Appleby Fair.

deputation of Travellers to Appleby Moot Hall for what proved to be the first of a series of meetings with local councillors and officers. There, by Wade's account, his 'eloquence' and 'forceful arguments', underpinned by 'many hours of hard work and deep thinking', turned the tide and ensured the future of Appleby Fair.

Figure 15. 8 June 1965, a roadside verge close to the Fair Hill. The press caption was: 'Capt. The Hon. Anthony Lowther and his mother, Muriel, Viscountess Lowther, talking to some of the campers, including Mr. William (Shocker) Bowman'. Photograph by Eric Davidson. Reproduced by kind permission of the Cumberland & Westmorland Herald.

The roadside tryst was captured on camera (Figure 15);[8] the minutes of the subsequent meetings survive. Boswell's key role is attested to not only by what others said but also by letters written in his own hand from his Lincolnshire scrapyard. But it is also clear from the evidence that the 'Gorgio authorities' were in reality anything but united in their resolve to end the Fair. Tensions between councils had been apparent in a testy exchange of letters over the removal of Fair refuse. The Clerk of North Westmorland RDC considered it the responsibility of the highway authority, which was the County; the Clerk of Westmorland CC had no doubt that it fell to the public health authority,

---

8   *Herald*, 12 Jun. 1965.

which was the District.[9] It is evident, both from the absence of mention of it in correspondence and from the defeated amendment of 30 April, that the County Council had not discussed the question of abolition with the Rural District Council before resolving to take action to bring it about. A week later the editor of the *Herald* wrote a leader condemning Westmorland CC's resolution as short sighted – 'ablution not abolition is surely the watchword': the New Fair, 'cleaned up and tidily gathered on a better site than the straggling roadside', would be a tourist attraction to match 'the famous gypsy gathering at Les-Saintes-Maries-de-la-Mer'.[10] When Westmorland CC Roads & Bridges Committee reconvened on 20 May, it was informed that letters of protest had been received from 'people attending the Appleby Fair', and that a meeting between a deputation of fairgoers and councillors from the various authorities had been mooted.

It is unclear how far ahead the Moot Hall meeting on the Wednesday of Fair week was planned. Heading a deputation of five Gypsy/Travellers, Gordon Boswell 'courteously but fearlessly' put his case:[11] he wanted to see Gallows Hill re-opened for the fair as a 'properly controlled site with charges', temporary toilets, a water supply and daily refuse removal. Present, along with four Appleby councillors and three officers, was one North Westmorland RDC councillor, accompanied by his council's clerk, who took the minutes and agreed to convene a formal meeting on 26 July, but made the point that the District Council did not have enough staff to clear rubbish on a daily basis.[12] Seizing the moment, Boswell on leaving the meeting immediately hired a loudspeaker van, broadcast to campers his version of events and appealed for cash donations; £165 was raised, more than enough to hire a local contractor to clear the verges. Michael Jopling, MP for Westmorland, was probably aware of the previous day's meeting when he toured the Fair on the Thursday, for most campers the day of departure. Having said what constituents wanted to hear in likening the scenes to 'Dodge City' and declaring himself 'horrified' by the 'dirt' and 'lawlessness', he significantly avoided any mention of abolition, merely saying that 'they would have to await the result of Westmorland County Council's action in taking counsel's opinion on methods of controlling the fair'.[13]

If the county authority was indeed already backing away from the implications of abolition before making any attempt to find out how that might be brought about, further incentive to retreat was provided by Appleby

---

9   Appleby Fair Bundle, letters between C. Howell and K. Himsworth, 7 Jan., 5 Apr., 6 Apr. 1965. A sign of mounting irritation was that they would address each other by surname only.

10   *Herald*, 8 May 1965. This gathering at a Mediterranean resort similar in size to Appleby, associated with Roma veneration of St Sara, continues to take place for two days in each May and October.

11   Wade mistakenly located the meeting at the Shire Hall, and surmised that 'Captain Lowther had a hand' in arranging it.

12   Appleby Fair Bundle, Minutes of meeting at Appleby Moot Hall, 9 Jun. 1965.

13   *Herald*, 12 Jun. 1965.

BC's regular meeting held on 16 June, the day after the *Penrith Observer* had urged the Borough and Rural District Councils to lay out 'a proper site' and quoted a traveller who had been 'going to Appleby all his life ... 10,000 policemen and all the County Councils in England won't stop us coming'.[14] During an hour-long debate on the Health and Housing Committee's recommendation to support the County Council, Councillor Arthur Taylor contended: 'If we do away with the fair, we are going to be reduced to a village ... for retired people', stressed the benefits to local businesses and argued that the campers could be accommodated on an improved Fair Hill. Dissenting voices included that of Councillor John Winter, a farmer and signatory of the 1960 landowners' letter, who asked rhetorically: 'We beat Hitler. Surely we can beat three or four thousand gypsies?'[15] Sam Burns, the Mayor, stressed that Appleby's representatives should go to the July meeting 'with a vote behind them as to whether the fair be continued or stopped'; and by seven votes to six an amendment that the fair should not be abolished was carried.[16]

The meeting on 26 July at Appleby Shire Hall, presided over by the vice-chairman of North Westmorland RDC, was held in private, but the minutes survive.[17] Arthur Taylor said that Appleby Borough Council would make the hill available for a one-week fair and was considering moving the rubbish dump. Gordon Boswell said that campers would pay, but wanted water and sanitation. He speculated that neighbouring farmers might also wish to apply for caravan site licences. Alan Fell, a local solicitor speaking for residents of Brampton, did not think – mistakenly, as later events proved – that they would. Anthony Lowther was among the county councillors present; he is not recorded as speaking, though he subsequently told the press: 'It would be morally wrong to stop the fair, as these people have always had a raw deal'. R.C. Howell, clerk to North Westmorland RDC, who took the minutes, said after the meeting: 'We all know where we stand now and can proceed to hammer it out'.[18] At the next meeting, held in the Shire Hall on 28 September to coincide with the preliminaries to Brough Hill Fair, with councillors and officers from the three authorities in attendance as well as senior police officers, a scheme 'to accommodate the campers on Gallows Hill for a temporary period of two years' was agreed. Boswell, at the head of a Campers' Committee of nine, promised that, in return for the use of the Hill rent free and with suitable sanitation, his committee would collect a fee from

---

14 *Observer*, 15 Jun. 1965. The *Observer*, which ceased publication in September 1968, had been conservative for most of its life and from c. 1930 to 1960 paid Appleby Fair little attention. But when the *Herald* tacked to the right, the *Observer* became more liberal; in the 1960s it gave the Fair sympathetic coverage.
15 *Herald*, 19 Jun. 1965.
16 Appleby BC Minutes, 1965-66, p. 16, 16 Jun. 1965.
17 Appleby Fair Bundle, Minutes of meeting at Appleby Shire Hall, 26 Jul. 1965.
18 *Herald*, 31 Jul. 1965.

campers and turn away any who would not pay.[19] 'Appleby Fair means so much to we people,' he told the *Herald*; 'we are highly satisfied'.[20] He claimed that this was 'the first time in history that a Gypsy man has been allowed to fight for his people'.[21] No one mentioned abolition. Westmorland CC Roads and Bridges Committee, which had set the ball rolling in 1964, noted without recorded comment the progress of plans by 'the three Authorities ... for providing adequate facilities for the Fair to be held on Fair Hill'.[22]

Progress was predictably slow: the County and District Clerks were still ready to argue over which council should pay £11.16s.4d for cleaning a road.[23] Not until February 1966 did a working party of 'technical officers' from the three authorities produce plans for the work to be done on Fair Hill to provide access, accommodation and sanitation for an estimated 459 caravans and 459 other vehicles; they estimated the cost of improvements at £2,200, and wanted to know how much the campers would contribute.[24] Boswell's handwritten response expressed alarm: 'it seems to me that you have gone far beyond the Amount to be spent on this Project from what we heard at the Meeting on 28 Sept 1965'. He would have to consult his committee, but 'my clients are all over the country at the moment'.[25] Nevertheless he headed north within a few days, and with five other Gypsy/Travellers in attendance assured six local authority representatives and a police superintendent that he would sell tickets at the gate, take responsibility for refuse removal, and provide accounts at the end of the fair, contributing 'any surplus towards the expenses of the three Councils'.[26] The Medical Officer of Health, Frank Madge, who had presided, wryly remarked on the 'most difficult circumstances' arising out of 'my inept chairmanship and gypsy verbosity', and concluded that 'all I can hope for now is that our Councils' palms will be crossed with silver'.[27]

It had occurred to the same meeting that under the 1960 Caravan Sites and Control of Development Act appropriate planning consent would be necessary for Fair Hill. Howell hoped that 'we shall not adopt too legalistic an attitude'.[28] Himsworth expressed astonishment that this had not been thought of earlier, before conceding that it would not be difficult;[29] and Appleby Borough Council secured planning permission 'for the use of Fair

19   Appleby Fair Bundle, Minutes of meeting at Appleby Shire Hall, 28 Sep. 1965.
20   *Herald*, 2 Oct. 1965.
21   Wade, 'Saving of Appleby Fair'. These words were not reported in the *Herald*.
22   WCC Minutes (1965-6), Roads & Bridges Sub-Committee, p. 635, 27 Oct. 1965.
23   Appleby Fair Bundle, letter from K. Himsworth to R.C. Howell, 14 Oct. 1965, returning NWRDC invoice.
24   Ibid., letter from R.C. Howell to S.G. Boswell, 9 Feb. 1966.
25   Ibid., letter from S.G. Boswell to R.C. Howell, 11 Feb. 1966.
26   Ibid., Minutes of meeting at Appleby Shire Hall, 24 Feb. 1966.
27   Ibid., letter from F. Madge to R.C. Howell, 4 Mar. 1966.
28   Ibid., letter from R.C. Howell to K.S.Himsworth, 3 Mar. 1966.
29   Ibid., letter from K.S.Himsworth to R.C. Howell, 10 Mar. 1966.

Hill during the Annual Fair'.[30] A more intractable worry was the likelihood that some campers would not go on to Fair Hill either because Boswell did not want them or because they did not want to pay. Two months before the 1966 Fair, North Westmorland's Chief Public Health Inspector gloomily predicted that 'quite a high percentage of the campers … will simply park on the roadside' and the expenditure of 'up to £3,000' would be 'more or less wasted'.[31] But the general verdict in the wake of the 1966 Fair was that these fears had not materialised. Most of the Fair travellers co-operated with Boswell – even if they did not all actually pay him £2 per pitch – in forsaking the roadsides for the Hill, now with a water supply and temporary toilets. The experiment had been a success.[32]

30   Ibid., letter from WCC to NWRDC, 29 Mar. 1966, quoting minutes of County Roads and Bridges Committee.
31   Ibid., letter from D. Calvert to R.C. Howell, 4 Apr. 1966.
32   *Herald*, 11 Jun., *Observer*, 14 Jun. 1966.

Chapter 11:

1966-1973: 'Completely Satisfactory'?

At a follow-up meeting in September 1966, both police and health officers reported that 'the transfer of campers from the highway verges to the Fair Hill site was completely satisfactory'.[1] In 1967, the verdict was the same: the Westmorland County Surveyor reported that 'arrangements on the Fair Hill worked very satisfactorily'.[2] Press reports were similarly positive, heaping praise on Gordon Boswell, 'the man they call the uncrowned king of the gypsies';[3] his reported verdict in 1968 was that 'We are very happy with the way things are going and feel quite a lot of progress has been made' (Figure 16).[4] In 1969, according to his biographer, under Boswell's 'good, spontaneous, almost anarchic administration', there were seven hundred trailers on Fair Hill, and police reported no trouble and no crime.[5] And Boswell eventually proved to be as good as his word in making each year out of the Campers' Account of which he and Captain Lowther were joint signatories, at least a modest contribution towards defraying the expenses of the local authorities. After the 1968 Fair, for example, the Joint Committee of the three councils was able to allocate £500 to Westmorland, £300 to North Westmorland, and £50 to Appleby, roughly a third of what the various councils had spent.[6]

The stability of the 'New Fair Project' was, however, illusory. It is a truism that 'Gypsies are unwilling ever to be, or appear to be, bossed around by another Gypsy'.[7] During the 1970 fair, in sweltering heat, there was a 'near-riot' on Fair Hill, supposedly triggered by 'a long-standing vendetta between gypsy families', and eventually involving fifty police officers.[8] In 1971 Appleby's Public Health Inspector reported 150 caravans on the verges of Long Marton Road, and 500 on the Hill.[9] It was becoming clear that Irish Travellers in particular were neither willing nor probably welcome to live even for a few days under the aegis of the Romani horse-dealer Bill Brough, to

1   Appleby Fair Bundle, Report of 3 Oct. 1966 by R.C. Howell on meeting at Shire Hall, 26 Sep.
2   WCC Minutes (1967-8) p. 461, Roads & Bridges Sub-Committee, 13 Jul. 1967.
3   *Herald,* 17 Jun. 1967.
4   Ibid., 15 Jun. 1968.
5   *Boswell*, p. 191, end note by J. Seymour.
6   Appleby BC Minutes 1968-9, p. 91, 9 Oct. 1968. In 1966 the councils calculated they had spent £2,426 between them; see Appleby Fair Bundle, letter of 23 Sep. 1966 from R.C. Howell to those attending Shire Hall meeting on 26 Sep.
7   M. Stewart, 'The Puzzle of Roma persistence: group identity without a nation', in Acton & Mundy eds., *Romani culture and Gypsy identity*, p. 86.
8   *Herald*, 13 Jun. 1970.
9   Appleby BC Minutes, May-Dec. 1971, p. 19, report by J. B. Cowdell, 14 Jun. 1971.

Figure 16. En route to Appleby Fair via the A66, c. 1968. Photographer unknown.
Reproduced by kind permission of the Appleby-in-Westmorland Society.

whom had Boswell had 'handed over the reins of leadership'.[10] It would take several years to confine camping to the fields; in the 1970s local authorities dug roadside ditches to make verges inaccessible; and simultaneously, as Boswell had predicted they would, local landowners struck deals that enabled groups of Gypsy/Travellers to camp with their own and avoid those whom they wished to avoid.

Meanwhile, differences within the stumbling troika of councils about both finance and the allocation of responsibility had soon resurfaced. In December 1966 a querulous note from Himsworth to Howell wanted to know why the County Council had yet to receive its share of the surplus on the Campers' Account, believed to be in the region of £750. He added his calculations as to the proportion due to each council: 191/250 to Westmorland, 47/250 to North Westmorland, and 12/250 to Appleby.[11] In April 1967 the cheques remained unwritten; Boswell promised to talk to Captain Lowther, but explained that no-one else on his committee wanted to be involved in organisation or 'handling Money'.[12] By then Howell had told Himsworth:

> I find it increasingly difficult to undertake any further work in arranging joint meetings because of staff shortages here and increasing pressure of

---

10   *Herald*, 12 Jun. 1971.
11   Appleby Fair Bundle, letter of 8 Dec. 1966 from K.S. Himsworth to R.C. Howell.
12   Ibid., letter of 10 Apr. 1967 from S.G. Boswell to R.C. Howell.

work. For this reason I think that I cannot hope to do anything further myself about convening meetings about the Fair, and I should be most grateful if you could do this through your Department. I think it is fair to say that I have borne the brunt for some years and that it is time someone else took a hand in it.[13]

Himsworth's reply was not without menace: 'I think it would be a pity to change horses in mid-stream ... I should hate to see ... me accompanying the County Council deputation to the Chairman of the Rural District Council alleging "unco-operativeness"'.[14]

Howell in turn expressed disappointment that 'you seem reluctant to accept a change',[15] and in the wake of the 1967 Fair tried another tack: 'I would suggest that, as this is the end of the two year experimental period, the three local authorities should consider whether experience shows that the Fair should be permitted to continue'.[16] Himsworth declined to be drawn on the suggestion that it was within the competence of the councils to award or withhold permission for the Fair, and merely responded that the County Roads and Bridges Committee was – in a striking turnaround from its position early in 1965 – 'agreeable' to the Fair continuing 'on similar lines to those which have operated during the two year experimental period'.[17] An informal joint committee of representatives from the three councils was set up to oversee the future management of the Fair, but North Westmorland RDC had already resolved that 'strong representations should be made that the organisation of the arrangements should be the responsibility of one local authority'.[18]

But which local authority? In November 1968 Himsworth advised Westmorland CC that it should rent or purchase Fair Hill, provided that Appleby BC or North Westmorland RDC would accept responsibility for the development and management of the site;[19] the Joint Committee endorsed the recommendation.[20] But ten months of negotiation proved 'unsuccessful';[21] the Rural District Council thought it was a good idea for the County Council to buy Fair Hill,[22] but Appleby was only willing to lease the site to Westmorland for the duration of the Fair, a maximum of eight days, with agreement as to

13   Ibid., letter of 3 Mar. 1967 from Howell to Himsworth.
14   Ibid., letter of 8 Mar. 1967 from Himsworth to Howell.
15   Ibid., letter of 10 Mar. 1967 from Howell to Himsworth.
16   Ibid., letter of 18 Sep. 1967 from Howell to Himsworth.
17   Ibid., letter of 17 Nov. 1967 from Himsworth to Howell.
18   Kendal Archive Centre, WSRD, North Westmorland RDC Minutes Book 15, p. 75, 4 Oct. 1967.
19   Westmorland CC Minutes (1968-9) p. 468, Minutes of Standing Sub-Committee 21 Nov.1968, presented to Roads & Bridges Sub-Committee, 12 Dec. 1967.
20   Appleby BC Minutes (1968-9), p. 141, 15 Jan 1969.
21   Westmorland CC Minutes (1969-70), p. 482, Roads & Bridges Sub-Committee, 16 Oct. 1969.
22   North Westmorland RDC Minutes Book, Book 16, p. 136, 4 Jan. 1969, Book 17, p 58, 29 Nov. 1969.

who would manage the site as a pre-condition.[23] Westmorland then, 'in the long-term interests of the Fair', explored the purchase of part of Warcop Range from the army,[24] only for the War Department to discover, after a nine-month delay, that it needed the land.[25] The County reverted in September 1970 to the attempted 'acquisition of Appleby Fair Hill site', but ran into the same obstacle. The Borough would not sell to the County, nor would it agree to a lease of more than a fortnight.[26] In July 1971 Appleby went further, resolving that it would enter into no arrangements with Westmorland regarding the 1972 Fair, the 'organisation and promotion' of which should be 'on terms and conditions to be agreed under the sole control of the Borough Council'.[27]

Within two months, however, it had backed away from this bold proposition, favouring instead North Westmorland's proposal for the re-constitution and formalising of a joint committee with three members each from County, Rural District and Borough councils.[28] Now it was the turn of Westmorland, which had a few months earlier had been pressing to buy Fair Hill, to stand on its head. In October 1971 Himsworth wrote to inform both Borough and Rural District that the County Council had resolved to withdraw from all arrangements for the Fair and was willing to write off the balance of money owed to it.[29] Both North Westmorland RDC and Appleby BC passed resolutions expressing concern at Westmorland's unwillingness not to accept future liability,[30] and in January 1972 the Town Clerk of Appleby pleaded with the County Council to 'co-operate at least for the 1972 and 1973 Fairs in view of local government reorganisation'. The County evidently relented to the extent of being represented at a meeting in May 1972 which concluded that in 1973 the Fair Hill campers must pay more.[31]

Behind these byzantine manoeuvres lay two pieces of parliamentary legislation. The 1968 Caravan Sites Act, a private bill introduced by the Liberal M.P. Eric Lubbock, with the backing of the Harold Wilson's Labour government, required County Councils by April 1970 to be providing accommodation for Gypsies, defined as 'persons of nomadic habit of life,

---

23   Appleby BC Minutes (1969-70), p. 74. 17 Sep. 1969.

24   Westmorland CC Minutes (1969-70), p. 489, Roads & Bridges Sub-Committee, 20 Nov. 1969; p. 505, Planning Committee, 17 Dec. 1969.

25   Westmorland CC Minutes (1970-1), pp. 189, 385, Planning Committee, 20 Apr., 16 Sep.1970.

26   Appleby BC Minutes (1970-1), p. 101, Council in committee, 11 Nov. 1970.

27   Appleby BC Minutes (May-Dec 1971), p. 32, Planning, Tourism, Publicity, Health & Highways Committee, 5 Jul.

28   Appleby BC Minutes (May-Dec 1971), p. 69, Planning, Tourism, Publicity, Health & Highways Committee, 6 Sep.

29   Westmorland CC (1971-2), p. 366, Planning Committee, 1 Sep. 1971; Appleby BC, (May-Dec 71), p. 120, letter from Westmorland CC, dated 20 Oct. 1971; North Westmorland RDC Book 19, p. 101, 3 Nov. 1971.

30   North Westmorland RDC Book 19, p. 149, 5 Jan. 1972.

31   Ibid., p. 243, 3 May 1972.

whatever their race or origin' who resided in or resorted to, their areas. Although discussions of this potentially explosive issue tended to be held in camera, it is highly likely that this was why Westmorland suddenly became interested in acquiring Fair Hill, and why Appleby insisted that the land was unsuitable for a permanent site for caravans, whether for touring or holiday purposes.[32] Hopes and fears that Fair Hill might, in County Council hands, become a permanent Gypsy/Traveller site were probably alike misconceived. Appleby was a special place to gather, not a place to live; and the economics of traveller life involved proximity to a much larger settled population – to whom services could be sold and with whom goods traded – than that residing in the environs of Appleby. But it is not hard to divine what was in the mind of the Appleby councillors who resolved in January 1971 that they would not transfer control of Fair Hill to Westmorland 'since the main use was, and would continue to be, agricultural'.[33]

In any event, in the course of 1971 the County Council changed its tune. In April 1970 a letter from the Ministry of Housing and Local Government had wanted to know what Westmorland was doing about provision of caravan sites for Gypsies, emphasising the need for public consultation.[34] Two months later a general election produced an unexpected Conservative majority and put Edward Heath into Downing Street. As it gradually became apparent that the new government was disinclined to put undue pressure on local authorities to comply with the 1968 Act, the County Council came to the conclusion that it could walk away from Appleby Fair. In part, too, this turnaround reflected the increasingly *fin de siècle* atmosphere in which decisions were being taken – or not taken. Since the publication of the Local Government Reform White Paper of February 1971, Westmorland had known that it was to be subsumed into Cumbria, an amalgam, based in Carlisle, of Cumberland, Westmorland, Lancashire North of the Sands, and the Sedbergh district of the West Riding of Yorkshire; North Westmorland Rural District would become part of Eden District, based in Penrith to which new authority would devolve most of the powers of Appleby, downgraded from the status of a borough to mere parish, though retaining the style of a town council. While shadow authorities moved into place in preparation for the new order to commence in April 1974, the old regimes faced the final curtain. On the evidence of its minute books, during last two years of its existence Westmorland CC chose to avert its eyes from Appleby Fair.[35]

32   Appleby BC (1970-71), p. 101, Council in committee, 11 Nov. 70. In April 2014 a former Borough
      Councillor confirmed to me what underlay the Council's reasoning.
33   Ibid., p. 145, Finance, Rating and General Purposes, 7 Jan. 1971.
34   Westmorland CC (1970-1), p. 189, Planning Committee, 20 Apr. 1970.
35   Westmorland CC Minutes 1972-3 p. 86, Roads & Bridges Sub-Committee, 3 Feb. 1972, refers to
      an impending meeting with North Westmorland RDC and Appleby BC 'with a view to discussing
      the future of the Fair.' No report follows. Westmorland CC Minutes 1973-4 do not mention
      Appleby Fair at all.

North Westmorland RDC, by contrast, 'resolved that Eden District Council be made aware of the problems associated with the Fair, and that due to increasing numbers of visitors each year, more accommodation would have to be provided for the parking of caravans'; it took the decision to spend £11,100 on three plots adjacent to Fair Hill amounting to twenty-five acres – Eden District Council 'to be informed'.[36] Meanwhile Appleby BC, unhappy at its imminent down-grading, mulled over which of its properties it would be practicable to withhold from the new authority, and – probably for the same reason that it had been unwilling to part with it in 1970 – decided that Fair Hill would be one of them.

Press reports give no indication that these behind-the-scenes manoeuvres had any impact on those at the cutting edge of the Fair. The 1971 'annual gathering of the swarthy-skinned gypsy and potter people from all parts of Britain' was reportedly deemed by the chairman of Appleby Magistrates' Court to be 'one of the largest but also one of the quietest they had experienced'.[37] The sunlit 1973 Fair, 'a busy and colourful scene, with fortune tellers doing a roaring trade, dealers selling everything from suit lengths to expensive china ... believed to have been the biggest ever',[38] was the last that would take place in Appleby as a borough in the county of Westmorland. We may be sure that few of the 7,000 – according to police estimates – 'gypsies and dealers' knew, still less cared, about the changing map of local government. The Fair would be there again next year.

36   Ibid., Book 21, pp. 39, 11 Jul. 1973, 73, 28 Aug. 1973.
37   *Herald*, 12, 19 Jun. 1971.
38   *Herald*, 16 Jun. 1973.

Chapter 12:

The Late Twentieth-Century Media Fair

The closure threat, exaggerated though it may have been, seems to have encouraged the attendance of Gypsy/Travellers from further afield. In 1969 the County Surveyor reported that there was such a 'considerable increase in the numbers attending the Fair' that the Fair Hill site could not accommodate all their vehicles.[1] In 1974 Bill Brough told the press of his pride in bringing London and Thames estuary Gypsies onto Fair Hill.[2] Michael Stewart has noted the Gypsy capacity for living 'with their gaze fixed on the permanent present', consigning the past to 'the homogenous, obliterating "some time ago"'.[3] The collective Gypsy/Traveller memory rapidly invented a back-history of generations of pilgrimages to Appleby Fair, impelled by a shared sense of spiritual commitment.[4] Boswell himself expressed his devotion to it in verse:

> But my father lived to ninety seven – I might just live to ninety eight
> Before I leave my old pals and seek Heaven's Gate
> And when that time comes I hope to meet the old dealers there
> And I hope they have a place to take me as happy as Appleby Fair.[5]

His editor was probably more accurate when he wrote in 1970 that the Fair had 'in very recent years become the most important meeting place for Gypsies all over Britain'.

Some Appleby residents still recall their enjoyment of the Fair's ambience. On Sunday afternoons they would mingle with the crowds of day visitors seeing the sights on the river bank or wandering on to Fair Hill, perhaps in search of bargains on trailers with a range of goods on sale that included Crown Derby pottery. Saturday night dances at Kirkby Thore, three miles away, drew crowds of both local and Gypsy/Traveller youth; anecdotal evidence recalls that there was no more 'bother' than at a typical village dance, with its desultory brawling; and that there were occasional sexual encounters between Fair boys and local girls, but never the reverse. In 1972, after a gap of six decades, Gypsy/Traveller infants again began to be baptised

---

1   Westmorland CC Minutes 1969-70 p. 324, Surveyor's report to Roads & Bridges Sub-Committee, 19 Jun. 1969.
2   *Herald*, 15 Jun. 1974.
3   Stewart, *Time of Gypsies*, p. 235.
4   *Boswell*, p. 194, end note by J. Seymour.
5   Ibid., pp. 113-5

at St Lawrence's, Appleby.[6] There is no obvious explanation for why Gypsy
christenings stopped, then re-started. Geoffrey Dixon, the incumbent who
carried out the 1972 baptisms shortly before his retirement, had been in the
living for nearly twenty years; a former mayor of Appleby, he had in 1965
sat on the Divisional Committee that recommended the abolition of the
Fair. Whatever the reason for the apparent change of heart, his successors
at St. Lawrence's would follow his lead in regularly baptising infants during
the Fair; and there were also Gypsy/Traveller baptisms and burials at Long
Marton church.

But despite these instances of mutual tolerance, there were contra-
indications of recurring dissatisfaction among the settled population. In the
early 1970s the letters page of the *Herald* was again a forum for complaints
about broken fences, fouled fields and 'our local common turned into
a cesspool', not so much by Gypsies as by 'hangers-on from the cities'.[7]
Appleby was being reduced to 'a complete shambles';[8] 'this annual invasion
of riff-raff' – not 'genuine horse-trading gypsies' – was 'a month of damage,
theft, filth, abuse and drunken orgies'.[9] Local unease was reflected in and
fed by press reports headlining the 'free-for-all', 'chaos', 'filthy mess' and
'spate of thefts', even though these were interspersed with others describing
a situation 'all quiet' and 'peaceful again', with 'little trouble'. Tenuous links
with local agriculture were further eroded with the closure of the century-old
Appleby Auction Mart, and with it the New Fair cattle and sheep auctions.

Commenting on the growing tendency of licensees and retailers to close
for the duration of the Fair, a 1980 *Herald* editorial speculated that, in
consequence of 'the charter granted for the fair so many years ago', Appleby
might become a 'ghost town'.[10] This prompted Peter Eggleston, managing
director of an Appleby builders' merchants with a shop selling hardware
and ceramics, to protest that the Fair brought 'a great deal of business';
the townspeople, having lost borough status and the assizes, 'do not want
to lose anything else'. In similar vein, Neil Ferber, occupant of a former
mill overlooking the shallows between a weir and footbridge where travellers
were accustomed to wash their horses, complained that the *Herald* served to
'promote intolerance ... fear and suspicion': the newspaper should instead
'try and help people understand that although the life style of travellers is
totally different from theirs, they are nevertheless human beings who come
here for their annual holiday to enjoy themselves'.[11] And indeed the tone of

---

6   Kendal Archive Centre, Appleby St. Lawrence Registers on film JAC 1717, entries for Jun. 11
      1972 and in June of most years thereafter. This development may have been a manifestation of
      the Evangelicalism identified by Matras (*Lucky People*, pp. 96-8) as 'especially widespread among
      Romani communities in America and Western Europe from the 1970s onwards'.
7   *Herald*, 24 Jun. 1972.
8   *Herald*, 23 Jun. 1973.
9   *Herald*, 15 Jun. 1974.
10   *Herald*, 14 Jun. 1980.
11   *Herald*, 21 Jun. 1980.

increasingly expansive coverage of the Fair did indeed become more positive again in the early 1980s, whether in response to criticism or reflective of a cycle of rising and falling tension.

In the absence of any figures other than police estimates of caravan numbers in the area, the accuracy of routine perceptions of increasing numbers of fairgoers is not easily assessed. Brough Hill Fair enjoyed a brief post-war renaissance, then declined in parallel with Appleby's surge to the extent that by the early 1960s only a handful of Gypsy/Traveller families kept the tradition alive there.[12] There was general consensus that visitors to Appleby Fair were proliferating to the point where spectators outnumbered campers. The most obvious explanation was the growth in media attention during and after 1965. In addition to the Cumbrian press, national newspapers carried occasional news reports and longer features in weekend supplements; and in 1972 the American *National Geographic Magazine* ran an article which described Appleby Fair as a 'cornerstone' of 'the foundation of the gypsy year'.[13] The broadcast media's relationship with Appleby Fair, apart from a radio North Home Service programme in 1954,[14] was confined to news reports until the late 1980s, but there was a developing genre of niche-published albums of photographs, with texts of varying merit,[15] as well as videos and DVDs intended primarily for sale to fairgoers and visitors.

Media coverage in the last three decades has often been roseate: the liberal-leaning press have seen 'the world's biggest gypsy party', a 'week-long jamboree' (Figure 17) with an 'infectious carnival atmosphere', characterised by the 'warm gypsy laughter' of 'wild-eyed Romany youths', 'brown-faced matriarchs' and 'husky blacksmiths stripped to the waist';[16] indeed, Appleby has been 'hosting scenes straight out of D.H. Lawrence at his lyrical best'.[17] By contrast, newspapers on the political right are more inclined to dwell on dirt, danger, cruelty and violence. In 2011 the *Daily Star* ran a series of stories anticipating a bare-knuckle showdown to determine the title of 'King of The Gypsies', to be held on Fair Hill with thousands looking on;[18] it never took place. Television-feature coverage of the Fair, most recently in Channel 4's *My Big Fat Gypsy Wedding*,[19] has inclined more to detached, faintly patronising observations of the foibles of all concerned. A BBC 2 *40 Minutes* broadcast in November 1988 featured a woman in an Appleby pub defiantly announcing a traditional Gypsy song, then singing "Are You

---

12   J.D. Marshall, *Cumbria Magazine*, Nov. 1974, pp. 280-2.
13   'When Gypsies gather at Appleby Fair', *National Geographic Magazine*, Jun. 1972.
14   *Herald*, 12 and 19 Jun. 1954: the programme, including location recordings, written by Richard Lloyd of Oldham, was broadcast at 10 pm on 24 June.
15   For example, W. Hall, *A Time to Come Alive* (Harrogate, 1976); B. Law, *A Time to Look Back* (York, 1991); J. McKale, *The Gypsies Then and Now* (2009).
16   *Independent on Sunday*, 2 May 1999.
17   *Guardian*, 9 Jun. 2006.
18   *Daily Star*, 5 Mar. 2011, 'Big Fat Gypsy Bloodbath'.
19   *My Big Fat Gypsy Wedding* , episode 4, 15 Feb. 2011, 'Bride and Prejudice'.

Lonesome Tonight" off-key, and a district councillor opining that the only solution to the fair's problems was to bring in the army. It concluded with shots of departing caravans and the voiceover, 'Appleby goes to sleep for another year'.

Such publicity only intermittently prodded local authorities into anything other than a purely reactive attitude towards an annual happening that was not theirs but could not be ignored. Cumbria County Council inherited Westmorland's desire to distance itself from the Fair as far as its policing and highways obligations allowed. Appleby Town Council had by 1974 decided that 'no action is necessary by this Council' because 'the responsibility for the New Fair rests entirely with Eden District Council'.[20] For Eden DC, based in Penrith, thirteen miles from Appleby across a county boundary that, albeit obsolete, lingered in the memory, the Fair was the mad woman in the attic – an intractable problem to be contained, but not talked about. Although the Environmental Health Officer would periodically speak to the press about the problems of Fair sanitation and rubbish clearance,[21] occasional discussion in the council chamber at Penrith was restricted to uncomprehending councillors complaining about the cost of the Fair to ratepayers and wanting to know why the 'organisers' did not pay.[22] A reconstituted Joint Committee of Cumbria, Eden and Appleby Councils, police and RSPCA saw its remit essentially as one of damage limitation.

In practice, the level of engagement fluctuated. Appleby Town Council, although reduced to parish status in 1974, retained its heritage, its mayor and some of its land, including Fair Hill. For the Fair's duration it continued to entrust its management and the collection of rent to a prominent Gypsy/ Traveller, although not without complaints that 'only about half' of what was collected reached the Council.[23] In 1984, in an attempt at a more positive approach, a Fair Hill committee of Appleby councillors and Gypsy/Travellers was formed; in 1985 the 300th anniversary of the imaginary New Fair charter was commemorated with a colourful parade through the town (Figure 18).[24] Succeeding years continued to bring contrasting perceptions: in 1987 an 'Appleby businessman' told the *Herald* that the fair was 'pure squalor'; a week later a local 'lady trader' said that this was 'totally unfair ... the gypsies have never caused me any trouble'.[25] At the Appleby TC meeting immediately following the 1989 fair, one councillor congratulated the police on a 'good job'; another said the policing had been 'disgraceful'.[26] Controversy was not confined to Appleby. In 1988 George Prall, former Green district

20   Appleby Town Council Minutes, 8 May 1974.
21   *Herald*, 11 Jun. 1977.
22   *Herald*, 7 Jun. 1986
23   *Herald*, 20 Jun. 1981.
24   *Herald*, 16 Jun. 1984, 15 Jun. 1985.
25   *Herald*, 6 Jun. and 13 Jun. 1987.
26   *Herald*, 17 Jun. 1989.

Figure 17. 'A week-long jamboree'. Photographer unknown. Reproduced by kind permission of the Appleby-in-Westmorland Society.

councillor for Kirkby Thore, alleged that his Conservative successor, Guy Nicholson, had organised a 'shameful' Ku Klux Klan-like operation of local vigilantes to evict Gypsy caravanners en route to the fair out of a field where they had been given permission to camp by a local landowner. The police had not been involved, and neither Guy Nicholson nor parish councillors wanted to talk to the press. The landowner's perhaps understated version of events was: 'They were just there for one night but villagers didn't really appreciate them being there so I just asked them to move on and they did'.[27]

On Fair Hill itself *Herald* reporter Dawn Robertson found in 1990

Figure 18. Celebrating an imaginary tercentenary; procession in Boroughgate, Appleby, 1985. Photographer unknown. Reproduced by kind permission of the Appleby-in-Westmorland Society.

27   *Herald*, 11 Jun. 1988.

'an air of sadness', with Gypsy/ Travellers 'defensive about any questions'; this she attributed to the effect of 'hordes of sight-seers'.[28] Two years later, she was more successful in securing an interview with 'the nearest thing you can get to a gypsy king', the eloquent and photogenic Billy Welch (Figure 19), filling the role previously taken by Gordon Boswell, Bill Brough and his own eponymous father. Described as 'one of the unofficial historians of the gypsies', he assured the reporter that 'they first started to come to Appleby after it was granted a charter in 1685 by King James II'.[29] In 1993 Billy Welch was in print again after refusing entry to the hill to New Age travellers in a 'convoy of ramshackle buses and vans':

Figure 19. Billy Welch on Fair Hill, 2004. Photograph by Keith Morgan; reproduced by his kind permission.

> People associate us all together, which is ridiculous … They are all living on the state, our people are workers … A lot of travelling people are reverting to the old, original name, gypsy, because they don't want to be associated with the sort who call themselves New Age travellers … anybody can become a traveller, but you have to be born a gypsy.[30]

In the absence of any further mention, it can be assumed that a New Age convoy was not what two middle-aged Irish Travellers, on their thirty-sixth visit, had in mind when in 1997 they expressed themselves happy that younger people were coming to the Fair; they were, though, troubled by the escalation of 'commercial business'.[31]

---

28   *Herald,* 16 Jun. 1990.
29   *Herald,* 13 Jun. 1992.
30   *Herald,* 12 Jun. 1993.
31   *Herald,* 14 Jun. 1997.

Chapter 13:

Managing the Modern Fair

By the twenty-first century retailing at the Fair reached a point where a whole 'Market Field', rented from a local farmer, was given over to traders in what, as ever, appeared to be a spontaneous development brought about by no directing force. Modern fairgoers continue to be compared unfavourably with their predecessors in the good old days.[1] Although the first of two violent and dispiriting pseudonymous autobiographical volumes by 'Mikey Walsh' makes no mention of Appleby Fair, the second asserts that it was an 'integral part of our year', until his family stopped going because it had been 'taken over by a different traveller culture, and the Irish travellers and the Romanies were never good at keeping peace with one another'.[2] The sociologist Margaret Greenfields, by contrast, observes that mutual tolerance, even intermarriage, between English Gypsies and Irish Travellers is becoming more common.[3] She argues that voluntary absence from a 'treasured social gathering' like Appleby would more probably be the outcome of some 'infringement of social codes', with the offenders effectively making 'public acknowledgement of their inappropriate behaviour' by avoiding 'contact with individuals or families with whom they are in dispute'.[4] There was certainly sufficient communication between all potential fairgoers to ensure that in 2001, as had happened in 1866,[5] the Fair did not take place because of the closure of access to pasture land in consequence of an epidemic of foot-and-mouth disease.

Periodically the appointment of official event managers has been mooted;[6] but recent litigation in the wake of an unfortunate accident pointed up the risks to any individual or body assuming such a responsibility. The police, County and District Councils had between them largely prevented the dangerous practice of horses being put through their paces on The Sands by designating a stretch of the road to Long Marton east of the hill a 'flashing lane', closing it to traffic for the duration of the fair and erecting fencing along the verges, from behind which the gallopers could be viewed (Figure 20). In 2004 a visiting spectator noticed an unattended horse on the verge, tried to secure it before it strayed into the flashing lane and sustained a kick to the

---

1   See Appendix 3 below.
2   M. Walsh, *Gypsy Boy* (2008), *Gypsy Boy on the Run* (2011), p. 290.
3   M. Greenfields, 'Family Community and Identity', *Here to Stay*, p. 56.
4   Ibid., p. 30.
5   *Mercury*, 9 Jun. 1866: Privy Council order prohibiting all cattle fairs.
6   E.g. *Herald*, letter, 18 Jun. 1988; Coles, May 2003. The suggestion resurfaced in 2012.

Figure 20. The 'Flashing Lane', 2011. Photograph by Keith Morgan; reproduced with his kind permission.

head which left him permanently disabled. He and his family sued Appleby Town Council on the grounds that it was liable because it promoted the Fair through its tourist information centre, and a recorder of Middlesbrough County Court awarded substantial damages. Appleby Council appealed and in 2009 three law lords reversed the judgement. Lord Justice Toulson – who was under the impression that the Horse Fair had taken place 'probably since the middle ages' – noted that the Appleby TC did not own the land where the accident occurred, 'nor did it cause or direct the various activities of the fair which took place beyond its own boundaries, including the tethering and racing of horses'; but his judgement, to which his two colleagues assented, was based on a broader principle:

> Many parish, town or city councils, county councils or regional authorities try in different ways to encourage and support tourism in their area (by which I do not mean land of which the body concerned is the occupier and therefore under a statutory duty of care to visitors). In many villages, towns and cities there are annual festivals of one kind or another. They vary in size from the small church fete or village show to big carnivals. I would reject the idea that those bodies, public or private, which try to encourage attendance at such events or undertake some

responsibility in relation to them thereby expose themselves to legal liability for the negligence of other bodies participating in the event.[7]

By the time the judgement was delivered another incident, whose implications were reputational rather than financial, had pushed the local authorities towards a less arm's-length approach. The 2007 Fair had produced a typically mixed reaction. Billy Welch considered it 'one of the best'; a police commander commented on 'another successful year'. By contrast, an Appleby resident thought the Fair had been 'an environmental disaster' with 'absolute filth' in the streets: 'if this was Penrith there would be a riot; because it is Appleby, it doesn't seem to matter'.[8] But these familiar tropes were drowned out by the outrage generated by the unfortunate drowning of a colt in the river Eden watched by hundreds, filmed and photographed as it happened, and speedily broadcast around the world. A Gypsy/Traveller from London, washing down someone else's animal, tried to bring it under control by forcing its head under water. The colt lost its footing, struggled frantically and, with its lead rope constricting its mouth and nostrils, had drowned by the time onlookers waded in and dragged it to the bank.[9]

The head of the local policing team was quoted in the *Herald* as stating that 'Gypsies and travellers have been washing their horses in the River Eden for centuries. It's part of folklore that washing their horses in the river gives them strength.' This highly questionable assertion was translated by the national media into a 'tradition of ducking each animal's head in the river'.[10] Websites devoted to animal rights urged incensed followers to demand a ban on this imaginary ritual; Appleby Town and Eden District Councils received a stream of abusive letters, emails and telephone calls. A particular target for threatening messages was the Chair of the Joint Fair Committee. On holiday overseas and unaware of what had happened, she answered a telephone call from a *Daily Mail* reporter, and later found herself quoted as saying: 'People have been trying to stop this tradition for years but it's part of history and is set in stone by way of a charter'.[11] Months of hate mail ensued.

The adverse publicity arising out of this incident helped convince Kevin Douglas, recently appointed Chief Executive of Eden DC, to depart from the strategy of his predecessors and take a more proactive stance towards the Fair. In late 2007 he inaugurated the Multi-Agency Strategic Co-ordinating Group (MASCG), which described itself as 'chaired by Eden District Council with support from representatives from the Gypsy and Traveller communities, South Lakeland District Council, Cumbria County Council,

7   *Solicitors Journal* 15 Dec. 2009, reporting *Glaister v Appleby-in-Westmorland Town Council* [2009] EWCA Civ 1325.
8   *Herald*, 16 Jun. 2007.
9   The perpetrator was convicted of animal cruelty at Carlisle Crown Court in March 2008.
10   *Mirror*, 12 Jun. 2007.
11   *Mail Online*, 11 Jun. 2007.

Figure 21. Horses in the River Eden, 2011 Fair. Photograph by Keith Morgan; reproduced with his kind permission.

Cumbria Constabulary, the RSPCA, Trading Standards and other agencies' with the aim of making the fair 'safe and enjoyable for all' (Figure 21).[12] It meets regularly in advance of and during the Fair for updates on potential and actual problems, maintains a website for public consumption, and has perhaps been as successful as it could be; it has certainly been able to provide accurate figures for caravan numbers instead of time-honoured guesses. A few weeks after the Fair, MASCG holds a public meeting, largely, sometimes exclusively, attended by self-selected members of the settled population from Appleby and surrounding settlements, at which grievances can be comprehensively aired. In 2013 the dominant theme was the prolonged occupation by those en route to the Fair of roadside verges in the nearby village of Sandford;[13] in 2014 it was disruption in Kirkby Stephen town centre, thirteen miles south of Appleby. There were renewed suggestions that there should be a transit camping area perhaps on part of Warcop Range, though it was doubtful whether the Ministry of Defence would be any more accommodating than it had been in 1970. Common tropes among Appleby residents are traffic delays, occupation of parking spaces, litter, the insanitary consequences of insufficient toilet provision, and late night noise.

12 Robin Hooper, Chief Executive of EDC, quoted in BBC News Cumbria on line, 6 Jun. 2013. This is a standard phrase.
13 A similar complaint had been voiced by Sandford Parish Council in 1967, but in 1968 the same source reported 'we had no trouble at all'. *Observer*, 20 Jun. 1967, 25 Jun. 1968.

Even with improved co-ordination and feedback there are pitfalls. In 2010, in the wake of over a hundred arrests and a stabbing at the harness race meeting the previous year and with rumours of retributive violence to come, the police made an operational decision to deploy officers in riot gear and mounted police. Additional supervisory demands placed on licensees led some to close their doors, and in Appleby's market place the Low Cross, a 17th century obelisk surrounded by steps and a favourite gathering point, particularly during the Fair, was caged off by the police without reference to its owners, the town council. An atmosphere of menace was widely perceived. On the Sunday afternoon several hundred Gypsy/Travellers followed Billy Welch through the rain in a march to protest against heavy-handed policing. Outside the police station he spoke eloquently to the television cameras;[14] and subsequently MASCG did acknowledge that mistakes had indeed been made.[15] Dot Anderton, Mayor of Appleby, whose council was unrepresented on MASCG, made a point of inviting Billy Welch to speak at the annual civic lunch a few weeks before the 2011 Fair, at which, with different police officers in command, a less confrontational strategy was adopted. A productive innovation was a review meeting each evening of the Fair between police officers, the Mayor and other local councillors, various members of the local community and a Gypsy/Traveller representative, at which specific concerns could be raised and addressed the following day. Coincidentally or not, reported affrays at the Fair have fallen since 2010. Although in 2013 police believed that a serious, violent incident had only narrowly been avoided thanks to effective intelligence work, arrests at the Fair also followed a downward trend.

---

14   BBC News Cumbria on line, 7 Jun. 2010.
15   BBC News Cumbria on line, 19 Oct. 2010.

Chapter 14:

Evaluation

Albeit united in a Gypsy/Traveller culture that enables them for a few precious days to dominate the space they temporarily occupy and regain a world otherwise rarely attainable, those who attend Appleby Fair are made up of diverse groups from diverse places. There is no more a directing organisation for them than for all the people who choose to spend their holidays in Blackpool or Torremolinos. The mood at the Fair depends on events: enduring equilibrium is probably unattainable. The response of the local population too challenges the truism that what you see depends on where you stand: from apparently similar vantage points, people perceive very different things, just as Leland and George Smith did. Stewart, inclining to the sociological construction of what makes Gypsy/Travellers, suggests that they are 'a part of ourselves, a part that we have difficulty acknowledging'.[1] The argument could be extended: perhaps the extreme revulsion among at least some of the settled population is the rage of Caliban at the sight of his reflection in the glass.

Credible membership of any social or cultural group requires that one is so perceived by at least two of three parties: oneself, other members of the group, and those who are not members. In wartime Eastern Europe, fascist regimes sought to identify Gypsies and eliminate them by mass murder; post-war socialist regimes attempted to create a socio-economic order in which no-one could – or would wish to – live like a Gypsy; neither succeeded. Gypsy/Travellers have survived and, for all their internecine quarrels, found common satisfaction in their moral and cultural superiority over non-Gypsies, whom they have perceived as being in thrall to mundane labour, acquisitiveness, reverence for authority and fear and suspicion of one other. Though it would be quite wrong to depict Gypsy/Travellers as immune from depression or substance abuse,[2] Stewart, who is not Gypsy but who lived among the Harangos Rom in Hungary in 1988-89 and documented his experiences and observations, concluded his study with their remarkable capacity for seeing themselves as truly free, able to 'live so "lightly" and "easily" in a world so full of heaviness and trouble'.[3]

Superficially, their collective persona could hardly be more different from that of another minority, who also suffered murderous persecution at the hands of the Third Reich and who have in the last half-century become a

---

1   Stewart, *Time of the Gypsies*, p. 237
2   Greenfields, 'Travellers' Health', *Here to Stay*, pp. 200-2.
3   Stewart, *Time of the Gypsies*, p. 246

significant element within Appleby's settled population: Jehovah's Witnesses. The Witnesses live unobtrusive, law-abiding, sedentary lives based on absolute faith in written texts; they knock on doors and set up stalls not to trade but to proselytise. They eschew any form of violence. Yet their social circle, like that of Gypsy/Travellers, is largely closed, entered from outside only with difficulty and on strict terms. Although Jehovah's Witnessses must engage with the outside world economically, they too are conditioned to view employment as a means to an end, not an end in itself. They share with Gypsy/Travellers an ethos of self-help, and place strict limits on their relationship with external authority and the wider community. They do not vote or join organisations. Witnesses, like Gypsy/Travellers, regard many of the issues that preoccupy their potential oppressors as simply irrelevant; although not immune to change, they remain convinced that theirs is the right way, and are proud of the inner peace that conviction brings.

Of course, mass gatherings of Jehovah's Witnesses, like that at the Leeds Arena in 2013, are not a charge on the public purse, requiring extra policing and refuse removal or the attendance of RSPCA officers. This is not true of Appleby Fair, which generates private profit at public expense. Hundreds of police officers drafted in, daily rubbish collections, portable toilets at strategic locations and much more, all come at a price. Attempts to compute the cost of the Fair are likely to be as inconclusive as speculative estimates about how much money it puts into the local economy. Some of the spending by public bodies represents diversion of resources rather than additional burdens, but local residents who complain that they are effectively funding the temporary disruption of their lives do have a point. However, the Fair has a continuous history of nearly two and a half centuries, and no one is obliged to live in its vicinity. Attempts to secure the Fair's abolition have foundered on the absence of any document establishing it, whose conditions might be shown to have been broken. Other than the improbable eventuality of an act of parliament specifically outlawing it, Appleby Fair could only be ended if every local landowner agreed on a self-denying ordinance not to lease their land to fairgoers, while the police and highway authorities simultaneously cracked down to prevent any roadside camping.

Even if this could be achieved, would it be remotely desirable? As those bent on ending the Fair discovered, the local settled population is far from unanimous in viewing it negatively, particularly when confronted with the prospect of having it taken from them. Apart from the significant element who benefit economically from the Fair, other residents, if they do not welcome it, at least accept it as part of the package of living in and around the town; 'it keeps Appleby on the map' is an oft-repeated mantra. In recent years Appleby Fair has been more widely recognised as having intrinsic virtue as a cultural occasion for an often-maligned ethnic group, reflecting favourably on the communities in whose localities it takes place. At the 2009 Fair students from Appleby Grammar School, which has an 11-18 comprehensive intake, carried out interviews with both Gypsy/Travellers and local residents, and discussed the event with classes at the local primary school. Out of this came a video and podcast, which the students presented to a teachers' conference "Community Cohesion and the Global Dimension" at the British Museum in November 2009.

There is, too, as the journalist Katharine Quarmby has pointed out, a strengthening spiritual dimension to Appleby Fair.[4] Gypsy/Traveller religious observance tends to be eclectic, but heartfelt nonetheless and more widespread than among the settled population.[5] For the past forty years Traveller children of various ages have received an Anglican baptism at St Lawrence's Church. The local Roman Catholic priest visits the Fair Hill, where caravans are often adorned with pictures of the Virgin. In recent years many families have befriended the retired Pentecostal pastor John McKale and been happy to pose for his fine photographic studies.[6] Another twenty-first century development has been the appeal to Gypsy/Travellers of the Light and Life evangelical church, some of whose pastors are themselves of Romani descent and who have identified their people as a lost tribe of Israel. In 2014 Light and Life revived a twentieth-century local Methodist tradition by holding an open air Sunday morning service on Fair Hill,[7] with a hundred or so participants. The proprietor of an Appleby shop selling 'collectables', including second-hand books, reported an unexpected demand for Bibles during 2014 Fair Week. But, as Katherine Quarmby notes, there is a potential tension between evangelical rigour – the paradox of nonconformist conformity – and the tradition among some Gypsy/Travellers of elaborate celebration of first communions, along with an abiding affection for candles, crucifixes and saintly images.

A less emotive approach to Appleby Fair might be to evaluate it in terms of what it contributes to the sum of human happiness. Gypsy/Travellers and visitors come year after year because they enjoy the occasion; and while there are undoubtedly residents who dislike the Fair intensely, there are others prepared to say that they enjoy it. In the early nineteenth-century the philosopher Jeremy Bentham postulated a 'felicific calculus': crudely expressed, that the worth of anything is most effectively assessed not by moralising, but by balancing the relative pleasure and pain that it produces. Safe in the knowledge that no mechanism for applying the felicific calculus has yet been devised, I conclude with the unmeasurable assertion that over time Appleby Fair would emerge in credit. But if it exists a hundred years from now, it will surely continue to be an unpredictable, volatile, controversial occasion and a magnet for mythology.

---

4   K. Quarmby, *No Place to Call Home* (2013), pp. 253-287.
5   Greenfields, 'Family, Community and Identity', *Here to Stay*, p. 48. Matras, *Lucky People*, pp. 95-100.
6   J. McKale, *A Century of British Gypsies* (2012) et al.
7   The Methodist mission to the Fair ran from the 1930s and 1970s, with some support from evangelically-inclined Anglicans. See Appendix 1.

Appendix 1:

Appleby Fair in the 1930s and 1940s

"As a young child in the 1930s I lived with my Parents at No. 15 Boroughgate and we had a Shop. I remember being quite excited as Fair Time grew near. Events were very rare in those days in Appleby so it was something to look forward to. They were mainly Horse drawn Covered Wagons in those days – I don't remember Vehicles pulling Caravans. The Gypsies all camped on the Sides of the road – along Long Marton Rd and round to Clickham and Croft Ends. There was nothing on Gallows Hill and no Stalls. But there was usually a Blacksmith with a Brazier to Shoe Horses. They all started coming on the Thursday morning when they were allowed to come for a week. The same Families came year after year and you got to know them. They would come down into the Town on their Flat carts in the mornings to do their Shopping and be greeted like old Friends. The women would all have long skirts and Pinnies on and their Black Hair tied Back under a Hed Scarf, and the children would be dressed in Colourful Frilly dresses and their hair in ringlets; I used to think they were lovely. It was mainly Vegetables and Bread and Basic Food stuffs they bought – but they were Friendly, Noisy and Honest. As I got older, 12 yrs onwards, we would go up on the 6 pm Ribble Bus my friend Jean and I, get off at Clickham and walk back and see the Gypsies sitting around their Camp Fires and cooking their Suppers. Wonderful smells of Wood burning and Food Cooking, and, of course, there was always a Fortune Teller, which was a great attraction.

By the 1940s it was War time and there weren't many Vehicles about, but the travellers still came. Sunday was Visiting Day, but there were no Cars or Bus loads in those days, but all the local People went from the surrounding Villages and it was a great day to meet old friends. People didn't travel far from their homes then, so it was quite an occasion. And on the Sunday Evening there was always a Service outside the Rising Sun (Figure 22). This was usually led by Mr Jackson, and there was Hymn Singing and Sermon's given by Methodist Lay Preachers. And everyone would join in and sing 'When the Roll is called up yonder – I'll be there'.

Then in the Evening the men (and some Women) would come down to the Pubs for their Beer. And you would often get a Strong Man entertaining at the Low Cross. He would have a huge Stone Slab on his Bare Chest and another would hit it with a Sledge hammer until it split in two. Or there would be an Escapologist getting out of Chains and people would throw them pennies. Then at 10 pm – Closing time, a crowd would gather to see

Figure 22. Sunday Fair service outside the 'Rising Sun', c. 1955. Photographer unknown. Reproduced by the kind permission of Appleby-in-Westmorland Society.

the pubs turn out, hoping to see a fight! There would be lots of shouting and laughter, and they would all scramble to get on the flat carts for a ride home. Tuesday and Wednesday were the main Fair days for selling horses.   They would trot them along the Sands and in the Market Square, from the Low Cross to the Post Office. And then on Thursday they were all away and the Hill was cleared by Noon.

Then after the War all started to Change. Cars started to be about and Bus trips came in and the Fair grew. The Old Days had gone – but I remember them."

Pam Kelly, July 2013.[1]

---

1   Mrs Kelly (b. 1929) has lived in Appleby all her life.

Appendix 2:

Appleby Fair in Verse, 1945

To Appleby
in Westmorland
I took a chestnut mare.

The roads dip in
the roads climb out,
the shallow river full of trout
sings, purls and ripples round about
its green cupped fields,
and there
they hold the autumn fair.

To Appleby
in Westmorland
by one, and two, and three
come strawberry roans
    and Cleveland bays
high-stepping hunters, Galloways
hacks, driving cobs, flea-bitten greys
from all the North Countree.

To Appleby
in Westmorland
come gypsy living-vans.
They've travelled from
the Downs, the Wolds
like galleons with bursting holds
of gilts and scarlets,
greens and golds
and brooms, and pots, and pans.

To Appleby
in Westmorland
come mugs and sharps and flats
and Shires that plod,
and colts that prance,
and girls as gallant
as a lance
and dealers hard of countenance
as their own bowler hats.

To Appleby
in Westmorland
I took a chestnut mare.

She'd mark of mouth,
her wind was sound,
I meant to sell . . .
I led her round:
I gave the farmer back a pound
for luck, when our clasped hands
    had bound
the bargain –
yet I swear
I almost wish I had not found
a buyer at the Fair.

R.C.S., published in *Punch*, 12 September 1945.[2]

2   'R.C.S.' was R.C. Scriven (1907-85), a regular contributor of verse. Whether or not he visited the
Fair, wrongly placed in Autumn, the Yorkshire-based poet may have heard about it – and the threat
to its future – from the long-serving *Punch* artist George L. Stampa, who had grown up in Appleby.

Appendix 3:

Gypsy/Traveller Memories

"Appleby Fair was the most important event on the calendar, a date not to be missed, a magical place where you met up with old friends and family; so many people waiting to greet you as you drove on, waving and shouting greetings on both sides of the road. Appleby Fair was never the same when old Gordon Boswell put it on the Hill, it lost so much of its charm, the days when you went from fire to fire all along the road to listen to some beautiful voices or talented step dances accompanied by music on a melodian. In those days everyone had a stick fire where most of the cooking was done, we brought over milk and water from the White House; those lovely people always welcomed us, even though we the young ones then, gathered there together every night to sing and dance. On Sundays the Salvation Army was always welcomed at the White House, us children would sing their hearts out, the catholic nuns would bless us from trailer to trailer for all the liberal contributions they received.

Unlike today, the only gorgies on Appleby were the visitors who usually came on a Sunday, but not in vast numbers and never, never as residents – that would have been unheard of and unwelcome. Appleby Fair was just for us, our main get-together, a romantic, magical place where you courted and met your future lifelong partner.

The media has got a lot to answer for the decline of this much loved place, before TV got involved all these so called travellers now did not know of its existence. Now every man and his dog wants to be a traveller, it makes me so angry, hence this letter, to read and see all these negative reports of piles of rubbish left and other complaints too sickening to mention.

Needless to say, Appleby fair is a distant memory for many others like me and my family, but never say die, my youngest grandchild was disappointed after spending just one day among all these hundreds of people, she said, "Granny, I never even met another traveller!" I could have told her that 98% on Appleby Hill were gorgios, none gypsy, who have no idea of the gypsy way of life, are completely lost when it comes to cleanliness – this is why they leave piles of rubbish behind, they think its ok to go unwashed; a lifestyle that would be very foreign to us. We are taught that cleanliness is next to godliness, you leave a place as you find it, the only clue you have been there is the dying embers of the fire.

I feel sad for my grandchildren who will never know the magic of Appleby fair, so many memories, friends long gone, my handsome husband of 52 years, one who made medical history as the longest survivor of a heart transplant, there will be a few residents of Appleby still around who can remember the days of my youth when we were welcomed every June."

Mary Burnside, 16 June 2013.[3]

---

3   Mrs Burnside, who lives in Darlington, wrote to me after seeing media reports of piles of rubbish left after the fair (see chapter 2). Her husband was a member of Gordon Boswell's original committee. A younger member of the family is an accomplished painter of traditional bow-top caravans. See J. McKale, *Gypsy Wagon Painters*, pp. 193-202 (2013).

Appendix 4:

St Lawrence's Fair

Like earlier sources, a '12th edition' of Ogilby's *Traveller's Pocket Book* with a map dated 1751 lists only the Whit fairs for Appleby. But a '2nd edition' from 1761 also lists St Lawrence's fair on 10 August for 'horses, sheep and linen cloth', as does the *Universal Magazine* of 1761. Thereafter St. Lawrence's fair routinely appears in Ogilby, Owen and Bowles, and in nineteenth century directories. There are no other clues as to exactly when in the 1750s, or by whose authority, it started.[4]

At some point the date changed to 21 August, or the Saturday nearest; and instead of linen cloth the main attraction in addition to livestock was cheese. In 1843 Boroughgate was lined by 65 cartloads of cheese, plus a few sheep and some superannuated horses: 'towards evening the old "tits" began to parade the street and though swapping went on briskly, buyers were scarce'.[5]

An 1878 report indicates a fair in decline. Sheep, lambs and 'a few pigs' were on offer, along with 'something over a dozen cartloads of cheese' clustered round the High Cross. There was only one refreshment tent, while 'spice and other stalls were to a great extent conspicuous by their absence.'[6] But in 1880 this 'at one time very important market for sheep and cheese', now described as Lammas Fair, mustered 20 cartloads of cheese, and was perambulated in the morning by the mayor and corporation and the town band; in the evening there was a 'promenade concert'. An 'efficient force of constables' was also in attendance; but 'such is the law-abiding character of the residents that their duties were absolutely nil'.[7]

Two generations later, 'mayor aldermen and common council in their robes, headed by a band of music, with mace and sword bearers and other paraphernalia' were still marking the occasion[8]; but by 1938, 'Appleby Cheese Fair ...with the coming of factories and other methods of disposal ... is now of a diminutive character'. Boroughgate would once have been 'lined with carts with tons of Wensleydale cheeses'; now there was 'only one exhibit', by

---

4   The Corporation Minutes make no mention of it; but nor do they of the short-lived wool and horse fairs of the 1830s and 40s.
5   *Mercury,* 26 Aug. 1843. 'Tits' was slang for broken-down horses.
6   *Observer,* 27 Aug. 1878.
7   *Observer,* 24 Aug. 1880.
8   *Herald,* 1 Sep. 1923.

John Parkin, a local grocer.[9] In August 1939 other matters preoccupied the press; if there was a St Lawrence's Fair it went unreported, and it has not taken place since.

Other than the 1843 press reference to the swapping of old horses, a typical Gypsy/Traveller practice but not unique to them, there is no evidence of their involvement in St. Lawrence's Fair.

---

9   *Herald*, 27 Aug. 1938.

Bibliography

Below is a summary of primary and secondary sources accessed in the writing of this book. For precise reference details, please see the relevant footnote in the text.

Documents

Appleby Borough Corporation (subsequently Appleby Town Council) Charters, Memoranda and Minute Books, Committee Minutes, Letter Books; also various legal documents.

Church Registers: Appleby St. Lawrence, Bongate St. Michael, Long Marton St. Philip & St. James.

Ledger of George and Matthew Atkinson.

North Westmorland Rural District Council Minutes and Correspondence.

School Log Books: Appleby British School, Appleby Council Central (later Primary) School, Appleby Grammar School, Bongate National School, Long Marton School, St. Lawrence's School, Appleby.

Westmorland County Council Minutes.

Almanacks, Directories, Magazines and Newspapers

Bowles' Post Chaise Companion

Bulmer's History, Topography & Directory of Westmoreland.

Country Life.

Cumberland & Westmorland Herald.

Cumberland Pacquet.

Cumbria Magazine.

Daily Mail; Mail on-line.

Daily Star.

Daily Telegraph.

English Chapman's and Traveller's Almanack.

Guardian.

Independent on Sunday.

Kelly's Directory of Westmorland.

Kendal Mercury.

Lancashire Evening Post.

Lonsdale Magazine.

Mannex's History, Topography and Directory of Westmorland.

Mirror.

Newcastle Chronicle.

Ogilby's Traveller's Pocket Book.

Owen's New Book of Fairs

Parson & White's History, Directory and Gazetteer of Cumberland and Westmorland.

Penrith Advertiser.

Penrith Observer.

Slater's Royal National Commercial Directory of Cumberland, Lancashire and Westmorland.

Solicitors' Journal.

Sun; Sun on-line.

Universal Magazine.

Westmorland Advertiser and Kendal Chronicle.

Westmorland Gazette.

BOOKS AND ARTICLES

Acton, T. ed., *Gypsy Politics and Traveller Identity,* (Hatfield, 1997).

Acton, T. & Mundy, G. eds., *Romani Culture and Gypsy Identity* (Hatfield, 1997).

Addison, W., *English Fairs and Markets* (London, 1953).

Atkinson, F.S., 'Gypsies in Westmorland', *The Kendalian* (1909), pp. 12-17.

Bonsall, B.C., *Sir James Lowther and Cumberland and Westmorland Elections 1754-1776* (Manchester, 1960).

Bonser, K. J, *The Drovers* (London, 1970).

Borrow, G., *Lavengro* (London, 1851).

Borrow, G., *The Romany Rye* (London, 1857).

Borrow, G., *Wild Wales* (London, 1862).

Boswell, S.G., *The Book of Boswell; the Autobiography of a Gypsy*, ed. J. Seymour (London, 1970).

Cameron, D.K., *The English Fair* (Stroud, 1998).

Carrick, T.W., *History of Wigton* (Carlisle, 1949).

Chartres, J.A., *Markets, Fairs and the Community in 17th and 18th Century England* (University of Leeds School of Economic Studies Discussion Paper, 1974).

Childs, J., *The Army, James II and the Glorious Revolution* (Manchester, 1980).

Clark, C. & Margaret Greenfields, M. eds., *Here to Stay: the Gypsies & Travellers of Britain* (Hatfield, 2006).

Clowes, M., *Appleby Fire Brigade: Johnny Rigg and the first Firemen of Appleby* (Kirkby Stephen, 2014).

Coles, G., 'Appleby "New Fair"', Appleby-in-Westmorland Society newsletter, May 2003.

Connell, A.N., 'Appleby in Westminster: John Robinson, MP', *Transactions of the Cumberland & Westmorland Antiquarian & Archaeological Society*, 3rd ser., vol. x (2010), pp. 217-236.

Connell, A.N., 'Blue Sky over North Westmorland: Appleby's Liberal Decade', *Transactions of the Cumberland & Westmorland Antiquarian & Archaeological Society*, 3rd ser., vol. vi (2006), pp. 195-215.

Connell, A.N., 'John Robinson (1727-1802), Richard Atkinson (1739-85), Government, Commerce and Politics in the Age of the American Revolution: 'From the North', *Northern History*, L.1 (Mar 2013), pp. 54-76.

Connell, A.N., 'The Domination of Lowtherism and Toryism in Westmorland Parliamentary Elections, 1818-1895', *Northern History*, XLV.2 (2008), pp. 295-321.

Connell, A.N., 'When and how did Appleby Fair begin?', *Transactions of the Cumberland & Westmorland Antiquarian & Archaeological Society*, 3rd ser., vol. xiv (2014) pp. 309-11.

Elvington, C.R. ed., *Victoria County History*, History of Gloucestershire vol. 6 (1965).

Ferguson, R.S., *History of Westmorland* (London, 1894).

Fraser, A., *The Gypsies* (Oxford, 1992).

Garnet, J.W., *Westmorland Agriculture* (London, 1912).

Haldane, A.R.B., *The Drove Roads of Scotland* (Newton Abbot, 1973).

Hall, the Rev. G., *The Gypsy's Parson* (London, 1915).

Halliday, P.D., *Dismembering the Body Politic: Partisan Politics in England's Towns, 1650-1730* (Cambridge, 1998).

Harrison, W., *Description of England* (1587).

Heelis, J., *The Tale of Mrs William Heelis: Beatrix Potter* (Stroud, 2003).

Hewitson, W., 'The Appleby Charters', *Transactions of the Cumberland & Westmorland Antiquarian and Archaeological Society*, 1st ser., vol. xi (1891), pp. 279-285.

Holdgate, M., *The Story of Appleby-in-Westmorland* (Kirkby Stephen, 2006).

Holloway, S.L., 'Outsiders in rural society? Constructions of rurality and nature-society relations in the racialisation of English Gypsy-Travellers, 1869-1934', *Environment and Planning: Society and Space* (2003), 21, pp. 695-715.

Holmes, M. R. *Proud Northern Lady* (London, 1975).

Hulbert, the Rev. N., 'A Survey of the Somerset fairs', *Proceedings of the Somerset Archaeological and Natural History Society, LXXXII* (1936), pp. 83-159.

Keet-Black, J., 'Gypsies didn't go to war – did they?' *Romany Routes*, vol. 7, no. 1 (Dec. 2004).

Kenrick, D. & Clark, C.,*Moving On* (Hatfield, 1999).

Kenrick, D. & Puxon, G., *Gypsies under the Swastika* (Hatfield, 1995).

Leland, C. G., *The Gypsies* (London, 1882).

Leslie, E., *A Gypsy Against her Will, or Worth Her Weight In Gold* (London, 1889).

Macaulay, T.B., *History of England* (London, 1848).

Mathews, Canon W.A., *Guide Book to Appleby in Westmorland and its Vicinity* (Appleby, 1890).

Matras, Y., *I Met Lucky People: the story of the Romani Gypsies* (London, 2014).

Matthews, J., 'Back where they belong: Gypsies, kidnapping and assimilation in Victorian children's literature', *Romani Studies*, 20.2 (Dec 2010), pp. 137-159.

Mayall, D., *Gypsy-Travellers in 19th C. Society* (Cambridge, 1988).

Miller, J., *James II* (London, 1978).

Morwood, V.S., *Our Gipsies in City, Tent and Van* (1885).

Nicolson, J. & Burn, R., *History of Westmorland and Cumberland* (London, 1777).

Okely, J., *The Traveller-Gypsies* (London, 1983).

Pincus, S., *1688* (Yale, 2009).

Quarmby, K., *No Place to Call Home: Inside the Real Lives of Gypsies and Travellers* (London, 2013).

Roebuck, P., 'Cattle-droving through Cumbria after the Union: the Stances on the Musgrave estate, 1707-12, *Transactions of the Cumberland & Westmorland Antiquarian & Archaeological Society*, 3rd ser., vol. xii (2012), pp. 143-158.

Roebuck, P., 'Cattle-droving through Cumbria, 1707-12: New Evidence from the Musgrave Estate, *Transactions of the Cumberland & Westmorland Antiquarian & Archaeological Society*, 3rd ser., vol. xiii (2013), pp. 256-260.

Scott, D., 'Recent Discoveries in the Muniment Rooms of Appleby Castle and Skipton Castle' *Transactions of the Cumberland & Westmorland Antiquarian & Archaeological Society*, 2nd ser., vol. xviii (1918), pp. 189-210.

Shaw, M., *Narrating Gypsies, Telling Travellers* (Umea University, Sweden, 2006).

Smith, G., *Gipsy Life, being an account of our Gipsies and their Children* (London, 1880).

Speck, W.A., *Reluctant Revolutionaries* (Oxford, 1989).

Stewart, M., *The Time of the Gypsies* (Oxford, 1997).

Thirsk, J. et al, eds., *Agrarian History of England & Wales* (Cambridge, 8 vols., 1967-1991).

Thompson, T.W., 'Affairs of Egypt, 1909' *Journal of the Gypsy Lore Society*, IV.4 (1909).

Thompson, T.W., 'Storms and Interludes', *Journal of the Gypsy Lore Society*, V.2 (1911).

Thompson, T.W., *Wordsworth's Hawkshead* (Oxford, 1970).

Wade, R.A.R., 'The Saving of Appleby Fair', *Journal of the Gypsy Lore Society*, XLV (1966), pp. 29-37.

Walsh, M., *Gypsy Boy* (2008).

Walsh, M., *Gypsy Boy on the Run* (2011).

Walton, P., *The Stainmore and Eden Valley Railways* (Yeovil, 1992).

Whellan, W., *History of Cumberland and Westmorland* (London, 1860).

Collections of Photographs

Hall, W., *A Time to Come Alive* (Harrogate, 1976).

Johnson, D., *Appleby Horse Fair* (2013).

Johnson, D., *Past Times at Appleby Fair* (2012).

Law, B., *A Time to Look Back* (York, 1991).

McKale, J., *A Century of British Gypsies* (2012).

McKale, J., *Gypsy Wagon Painters* (2013).

McKale, J., *The Gypsies Then and Now* (2009).

McKale, J., *The Tilly Wool Story: Extracts from the life of a Romany Gypsy* (2009).

Sagar-Musgrave, R., *Appleby Fair: the Greatest Gypsy and Traveller Gathering* (London, 2011).

Sands, H.M., *Absolutely Appleby* (Ipswich 2013).

Sands, H.M., *The Horses of Appleby Fair* (Ipswich 2011).

Index